ZAGAT

New Jersey Shore Restaurants

2012/13

LOCAL EDITOR
Pat Tanner

STAFF EDITOR
Yoji Yamaguchi with Curt Gathje

Published and distributed by
Zagat Survey, LLC
76 Ninth Avenue
New York, NY 10011
T: 212.977.6000
E: newjersey@zagat.com
www.zagat.com

ACKNOWLEDGMENTS

We thank Mike Lima and Rosie Saferstein, as well as the following members of our staff: Caitlin Miehl (editor), Anna Hyclak (editor), Brian Albert, Sean Beachell, Maryanne Bertollo, Katie Carroll, Reni Chin, Larry Cohn, Nicole Diaz, Kelly Dobkin, Jeff Freier, Alison Gainor, Matthew Hamm, Justin Hartung, Marc Henson, Ryutaro Ishikane, Natalie Lebert, Mike Liao, Vivian Ma, James Mulcahy, Polina Paley, Amanda Spurlock, Chris Walsh, Jacqueline Wasilczyk, Sharon Yates, Anna Zappia and Kyle Zolner.

The reviews in this guide are based on public opinion surveys. The ratings reflect the average scores given by the survey participants who voted on each establishment. The text is based on quotes from, or paraphrasings of, the surveyors' comments. Phone numbers, addresses and other factual data were correct to the best of our knowledge when published in this guide.

What's New

LET THE REVELS BEGIN: Michel Richard is part of a posse of nationally acclaimed toques opening restaurants in the Revel resort and casino in 2012. Ready to open at press time are his poolside **O Bistro & Wine Bar** and his mornings-only **Breakfast Room.** (His more formal **Central Michel Richard** is not far behind.) DC chef Robert Wiedmaier (**Marcel's**) is also in the game with his Belgian gastropub, **Mussel Bar.** Following these to the tables will be a trio by Jose Garces (**Amada, Village Whiskey, Distrito Cantina**), *Iron Chef* Marc Forgione's **American Cut** steakhouse, Alain Allegretti's **Azure by Allegretti** and a branch of the NY cafe **Lugo.**

AC'S HIGH: Revel's inside straight isn't causing AC's other casinos to fold, however. Harrah's is home to a grand new sibling of **Luke Palladino,** the Northfield Italian bearing its chef's name, as well as the BR Guest group's Mexican cantina, **Dos Caminos.** Chris Scarduzio, a veteran of **Mia** at Caesars (with Georges Perrier), is on board at the Showboat with his steakhouse, **Scarduzio's,** while West Coast chef Kerry Simon has checked into the Hilton with his casual seasonal steakhouse, **Simon Prime.**

ROCK ON: Shore native Jon Bon Jovi hits the foodie stage with his nonprofit community restaurant, **JBJ Soul Kitchen,** in Red Bank, where diners pay what they can afford for an American homestyle meal, or else perform volunteer work. For those who prefer a Latin beat (and an ocean view), **Cubacan** brings South Beach to the Asbury Park boardwalk. Meanwhile, chef John Schatz of Cape May's highly rated **Union Park Dining Room** comes out for an encore in Wildwood with **Pacific Grill.**

MAKE SHORE IT'S OPEN: While a good number of Shore restaurants are open year-round, others close or have limited hours during the off-season. Any time of year, it's best to phone ahead to confirm availability.

Princeton, NJ   Pat Tanner
May 9, 2012

Top Food

<u>29</u> Nicholas | *American*

<u>28</u> Washington Inn | *American*
Bay Ave. Tratt. | *Amer./Italian*

<u>27</u> Drew's Bayshore | *American*
Whispers | *American*
Old Homestead | *Steak*
Il Mulino NY | *Italian*
Yellow Fin | *American*

<u>26</u> Belford Bistro | *American*
Piccola Italia | *Italian*
Yumi | *Asian*
Ebbitt Room | *American*
Chef Vola's | *Italian*
White House | *Sandwiches*
Girasole | *Italian*
410 Bank St. | *Caribbean/Creole*
Dock's Oyster | *Seafood*
Black Duck | *Eclectic*
Mia | *Italian*
Peter Shields* | *American*
SeaBlue | *Seafood*
Buddakan | *Asian*
Atlantic B&G | *Amer./Seafood*

<u>25</u> Little Saigon | *Vietnamese*
Moonstruck | *Amer./Med.*

Union Park | *American*
Steve & Cookie's | *American*
Taka | *Japanese*
David Burke | *American*
Navesink Fishery* | *Seafood*
Morton's Steak | *Steak*
Bobby Flay Steak | *Steak*
Ruth's Chris | *Steak*
Capriccio | *Italian*
Palm | *Steak*
Trinity | *American*
Le Fandy | *French*
Sono Sushi | *Japanese*
Tisha's* | *American*
Labrador | *Eclectic*
Ikko | *Japanese*
Tomatoes | *Californian/Eclectic*
Sage | *Mediterranean*
West Lake Seafood | *Chinese*
Dish | *American*

<u>24</u> Raimondo's | *Italian*
Fornelletto | *Italian*
Kanji | *Japanese*
Plan B | *American*
Mustache Bill's | *Diner*

---

* Indicates a tie with restaurant above; excludes places with low votes

Vote at zagat.com

TOP FOOD

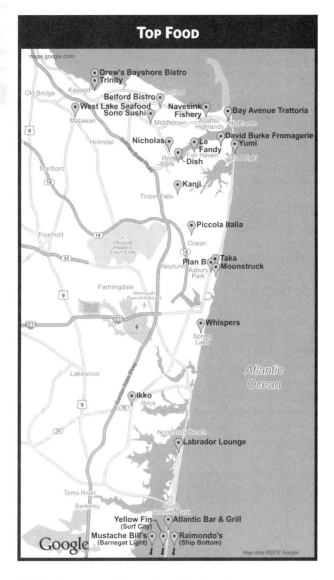

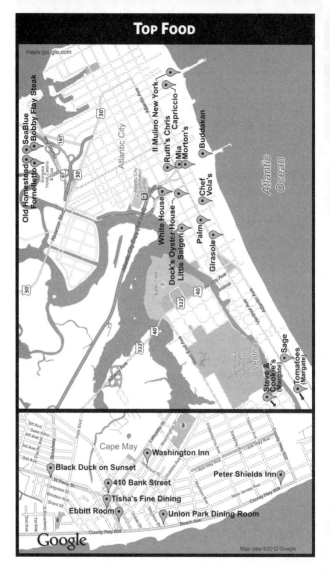

maps.google.com

Atlantic City

Il Mulino New York
Ruth's Chris
Mia
Morton's
Capriccio
Buddakan

Atlantic Ocean

Old Homestead
SeaBlue
Bobby Flay Steak
Fornelletto
Borgata Hotel Casino & Spa

Chef Vola's
White House
Dock's Oyster House
Little Saigon
Palm
Girasole

Ventnor

Sage
Tomatoes (Margate)
Steve & Cookie's (Margate)

Cape May

Washington Inn
Black Duck on Sunset
410 Bank Street
Peter Shields Inn
Tisha's Fine Dining
Ebbitt Room
Union Park Dining Room

Google

Map data ©2012 Google

Ratings & Symbols

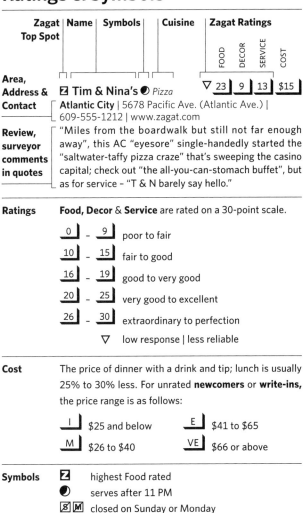

	Zagat Top Spot	Name	Symbols		Cuisine	Zagat Ratings			
						FOOD	DECOR	SERVICE	COST

Area, Address & Contact

🅩 **Tim & Nina's** ◑ *Pizza*

▽ 23 | 9 | 13 | $15

Atlantic City | 5678 Pacific Ave. (Atlantic Ave.) | 609-555-1212 | www.zagat.com

Review, surveyor comments in quotes

"Miles from the boardwalk but still not far enough away", this AC "eyesore" single-handedly started the "saltwater-taffy pizza craze" that's sweeping the casino capital; check out "the all-you-can-stomach buffet", but as for service – "T & N barely say hello."

Ratings   **Food, Decor** & **Service** are rated on a 30-point scale.

0 – 9   poor to fair

10 – 15   fair to good

16 – 19   good to very good

20 – 25   very good to excellent

26 – 30   extraordinary to perfection

▽   low response | less reliable

Cost   The price of dinner with a drink and tip; lunch is usually 25% to 30% less. For unrated **newcomers** or **write-ins,** the price range is as follows:

I $25 and below   E $41 to $65

M $26 to $40   VE $66 or above

Symbols   🅩   highest Food rated

◑   serves after 11 PM

🅢 🅜   closed on Sunday or Monday

⌿   no credit cards accepted

RESTAURANT
DIRECTORY

	FOOD	DECOR	SERVICE	COST

Aamantran ⓜ *Indian* ▽ | 21 | 15 | 20 | $26

Toms River | Victoria Plaza | 1594 Rte. 9 S. (Church Rd.) | 732-341-5424

In Hindi, the name means 'invitation' and this Indian BYO in a Toms River strip mall draws diners with its clay ovens, Bollywood soundtrack and "large selection" of "very good" vittles; "friendly" staffers willing to "answer any questions" and "inspiring" lunch buffets add to its appeal.

Aby's *Mexican* | 20 | 11 | 18 | $23

Matawan | 141 Main St. (Little St.) | 732-583-9119

Proponents praise the "fresh", "simple" Mexican food "done well" at this "humble" "neighborhood" BYO in Downtown Matawan; sure, the interior's strictly "bare-bones" and the service "inconsistent", but the portions are "generous", the prices "comfortable" and there's a guitarist on Saturday nights in the summer.

Aligado *Thai* ▽ | 24 | 16 | 20 | $26

Hazlet | 2780 Rte. 35 (Miller Ave.) | 732-888-7568

Chef-owner George Zhenz is "always around" at this BYO "hidden gem" secreted in a "trailerlike building" on Route 35 in Hazlet; "to-die-for" sushi, "tasty" Thai food and "friendly" service make the "tired" decor easier to overlook.

Allen's Clam Bar ⓜ *Seafood* ▽ | 22 | 11 | 21 | $21

New Gretna | 5650 Rte. 9 (bet. Frenchs Ln. & Rte. 679) | 609-296-4106

"Clams!" – think half-shell, steamed, Casino – keep locals coming back to this "popular", no-frills BYO in New Gretna that also slings "basic fried seafood"; granted, there's "not much decor" and it's "always jammed in the summer", but at least service is "fast" and the price is right.

Alps Bistro ⓜ *German* | - | - | - | M

Allentown | 4 S. Main St. (Church Rd.) | 609-223-0335

The eight tables of this modest BYO German in Allentown fill up fast, thanks to its reliable, affordable wursts, schnitzels and strudels, as well as Eastern European faves such as kielbasa and chicken paprikash, which are served by friendly owners in a homey space adorned with children's artwork; open for lunch daily, it serves dinner Thursdays–Saturdays and breakfast on weekends.

Angelo's Fairmount Tavern *Italian*

21 | 15 | 20 | $33

Atlantic City | 2300 Fairmount Ave. (Mississippi Ave.) | 609-344-2439 | www.angelosfairmounttavern.com

For a "respite" from Atlantic City's "huge casino restaurants", insiders eschew the boardwalk for this "old-fashioned" Italian, now in its eighth decade, where the Mancuso family "makes you feel at home" with "mama's-in-the-kitchen" "red-gravy" cooking and "no-nonsense" service; despite "kitschy decor" and a no-reservations policy, most agree everything's "still solid" here.

Anjelica's ▤ *Italian*

24 | 17 | 20 | $44

Sea Bright | 1070 Ocean Ave. (bet. Peninsula Ave. & River St.) | 732-842-2800 | www.anjelicas.com

An "angel must be in the kitchen" of this "bustling" Southern Italian BYO in Sea Bright, a "real find" on the Jersey Shore, where the "heavenly" food and "skilled service" offset the "raucous atmosphere", "tight tables" and "long waits", even with reservations.

Anna's Italian Kitchen ▤ *Italian*

23 | 17 | 21 | $43

Middletown | Fountain Ridge Shopping Ctr. | 1686 Rte. 35 S. (Old Country Rd.) | 732-275-9142 | www.annasitaliankitchen.com

"Hands-on" chef Anna Perri produces "fine Italian food" (think "unmatchable" gnocchi, "excellent" linguini) at this "tasty" BYO parked in an "obscure strip mall" in Middletown; too bad about the "blah" decor and somewhat "expensive" pricing, but at least the service is "lovely."

NEW Aqua Blu Kitchen & Cocktails *American*

- | - | - | E

Toms River | 3410 Rte. 37 E. (Bridge St.) | 732-270-1180 | www.aquablukitchen.com

The sprawling space boasting multiple dining rooms, two bars and a lounge suits the wide range of New American offerings (from crudo to sliders) at this spendy Toms River eatery located at the foot of the bridge that leads to Seaside; there are sunset views from the outdoor patio and live music on weekends.

| | FOOD | DECOR | SERVICE | COST |

Athenian Garden Ⓜ *Greek*
| | 23 | 15 | 19 | $28 |

Galloway Township | 619 S. New York Rd. (bet. Brook Ln. & Holly Brook Rd.) | 609-748-1818 | www.athenian-garden.com
"Bringing Greece to Galloway", this Hellenic BYO serves a "reasonably priced" "quality" menu in a "tucked-away" setting; the "plain" decor is trumped by a "homey" ambiance and "welcoming" staffers.

Atlantic Bar & Grill Ⓜ *American/Seafood*
| | 26 | 22 | 23 | $51 |

South Seaside Park | Central & 24th Aves. (J St.) | 732-854-1588 | www.atlanticbarandgrillnj.com
Views of "crashing waves" and "dune grass blowing in the breeze" supply the atmosphere at this oceanside American seafooder in South Seaside Park where the "delectable" cooking is a match for the "majestic" vistas from its floor-to-ceiling windows; just ignore the "seedy" exterior and get there "early" – "long waits" are the norm here.

Avenue *French*
| | 22 | 27 | 21 | $52 |

Long Branch | Pier Vill. | 23 Ocean Ave. (bet. Chelsea Ave. & Laird St.) | 732-759-2900 | www.leclubavenue.com
"Unusually sophisticated for the Jersey Shore", this "gorgeous" French brasserie in Long Branch's Pier Village boasts "delicious" food, "stylish" decor, "sweeping" ocean views and a "scene-and-a-half" vibe; "pretty-penny" pricing and "attitude" from the otherwise "professional" staff come with the territory.

Avon Pavilion *American*
| | 19 | 18 | 20 | $30 |

Avon-by-the-Sea | 600 Ocean Ave. (bet. Norwood & Woodland Aves.) | 732-775-1043 | www.avonpavilion.com
Aka the "Av Pav", this seasonal boardwalk BYO in Avon is best known for its "awesome" ocean panoramas, "summer breezes" and "upbeat" "college-kid servers"; given that the "basic" American food on offer is "nothing extraordinary", its "main asset is the location."

Axelsson's Blue Claw *Seafood*
| | 23 | 21 | 23 | $48 |

Cape May | 991 Ocean Dr. (Rte. 109) | 609-884-5878 | www.blueclawrestaurant.com
Located "off the beaten path" in the Cape May boatyard, this seasonal seafooder dishes out "quality" dinners, which are served by an

"exceptionally nice" team in a "linen-tablecloth" setting; though the food's "not haute cuisine", it's "reliable" enough and certainly "fresh", given that local fishermen "deliver their catch" right outside the door.

Bahrs Landing *Seafood*

17 | 16 | 18 | $38

Highlands | 2 Bay Ave. (Highland Ave.) | 732-872-1245 | www.bahrslanding.com

This "nothing-fancy" seafooder overlooking Sandy Hook Bay has been a Highlands "classic" since 1917; fans say its "simple" traditional fare – especially the lobster – "couldn't get any fresher", though critics contend the "just ok" grub and "welcome-to-1960" decor "could use more spice."

NEW Baia *Italian*

- | - | - | E

Somers Point | 998 Bay Ave. (Goll Ave.) | 609-926-9611 | www.baiarestaurant.com

Views of Great Egg Harbor Bay and boats pulling up to the dock next to its multilevel decks are part of the attraction of this sprawling Somers Point seasonal; three bars, live entertainment and an upscale, traditional Italian menu with an emphasis on seafood complete the picture.

Baja Fresh Mexican Grill *Mexican*

17 | 11 | 15 | $12

Union Township | 2311 Rte. 66 (Neptune Blvd.) | Ocean Township | 732-493-5300 | www.bajafresh.com

Somewhat "upscale fast food" that's "relatively healthy" and "as fresh as the name implies" is the concept at this Mexican chain link in Union Township that may not be "what you get in Mexico" but is "tasty" all the same; it also appeals to "budget-minded" types since it's "hard to beat for the price."

Bamboo Leaf ⓜ *Thai/Vietnamese*

22 | 16 | 19 | $29

Bradley Beach | 724 Main St. (McCabe Ave.) | 732-774-1661

They "try hard" at this bamboo-bedecked Bradley Beach Southeast Asian BYO serving "reasonably authentic" Thai and Vietnamese cuisines; service is "efficient", and while the decor is "lackluster", at least the price tag is "low."

	FOOD	DECOR	SERVICE	COST

Barnacle Bill's ● *Burgers*   22 | 16 | 19 | $28

Rumson | 1 First St. (River Rd.) | 732-747-8396 |
www.barnaclebillsrumson.com

"Mouthwatering" hamburgers are the star of the show at this
"fun" Rumson "dump" located along the Navesink River, a "super-
casual" place where patrons "watch Sunday football" and toss their
"peanut shells on the floor"; despite a "noisy" sound level, "corny
nautical decor" and "slow" service, it's usually a "mob scene", so
"plan on waiting."

Barrels *Italian*   21 | 14 | 19 | $31

Linwood | 199 New Rd. (Central Ave.) | 609-926-9900 🖪
Margate | 9 S. Granville Ave. (bet. Atlantic & Ventnor Aves.) |
609-823-4400
www.barrelsfoods.com

These "reasonably priced" "homestyle" Italians in the Shore towns
of Linwood and Margate are quintessential "neighborhood" BYOs
with "classic" *cucina* and "neighborhood" vibes; since there's "no atmosphere" in evidence, many opt for "takeout."

Basil T's *American/Italian*   20 | 20 | 20 | $37

Red Bank | 183 Riverside Ave. (Maple Ave.) | 732-842-5990 |
www.basilt.com

Red Bank's "popular" brewpub is known for its "sociable"
atmosphere – especially in the "lively" bar – along with "solid"
Italian-American comfort vittles washed down with "great" house
beers; the "super-friendly" staff is a plus, but many report it's "too
pricey for what it is."

Bay Avenue Trattoria 🅼 *American/Italian*   28 | 13 | 23 | $44

Highlands | 122 Bay Ave. (Cornwall St.) | 732-872-9800 |
www.bayavetrattoria.com

"Creative chef" Joe Romanowski and "fabulous host" Maggie
Lubcke supply the "magic" at this "unassuming" Italian-American
BYO in Highlands where "divinely prepared" dishes and "tiny" dimensions make reservations "a must any night of the week"; though
the decor is "nonexistent", few notice since the "emphasis is on
the food" here.

⚡ Belford Bistro *American*

26 | 19 | 23 | $45

Belford | 870 Main St. (Maple Ave.) | 732-495-8151 |
www.belfordbistro.com

"Shore foodies" head for an "out-of-the-way" Belford strip mall to sample the New American "culinary artistry" of chefs Kurt Bomberger and Crista Trovato at this "intimate", "New York City-quality" BYO; the staff "knows their food", weekday bargain prix fixes bring costs down and, no surprise, it's "harder to get into than in the past."

Bella Sogno Ⓜ *Italian*

21 | 18 | 18 | $34

Bradley Beach | 600 Main St. (Brinley Ave.) | 732-869-0700 |
www.bellasognorestaurant.com

It may be parked on a "side street" in Bradley Beach, but the Italian cooking is decidedly "Main Street" at this "reliable" Shore BYO where the prices are "reasonable" and "reservations should be made in advance."

Benihana *Japanese*

18 | 18 | 19 | $38

Toms River | Ocean County Mall | 1201 Hooper Ave. (Oak Ave.) |
732-736-7071 | www.benihana.com

At this Toms River link of the "original" teppanyaki chain, "swift knives" and "decent showmanship" from the chefs make for "entertaining" meals with the kids, even if the flavors can be "hit-or-miss"; there's "no intimate dining here", but then again the "distracting" "floor show" can be a "good thing" "if you don't like the person you're with."

Berkeley Restaurant & Fish Market *Seafood*

∇ 20 | 12 | 18 | $28

South Seaside Park | Central & 24th Aves. (J St.) | 732-793-0400 |
www.berkeleyrestaurantandfishmarket.com

This "typical" seasonal seafooder in South Seaside Park has been reeling in "quality" fin fare since 1925, and dishing it out in "sizable" portions for "reasonable" tabs; 360-degree sightlines of Barnegat Bay from the top floor and "obliging" attendants distract from the lack of decor.

	FOOD	DECOR	SERVICE	COST

Bienvenue ☑ *French*
| 22 | 19 | 21 | $48 |

Red Bank | 7 E. Front St. (Wharf Ave.) | 732-936-0640 |
www.bienvenuerestaurant.com

For a "bit of the Left Bank" in Red Bank, try this "sweet", "petite" bistro that charms fans with its "classic" French cooking, "comfortable" cafe decor and "attentive" staffers; prices skew "high", but $30 prix fixe dinners Tuesdays–Thursdays and a BYO policy "help keep the final tab within reason."

Big Ed's BBQ *BBQ*
| 18 | 11 | 17 | $25 |

Matawan | 305 Rte. 34 N. (Disbrow Rd.) | 732-583-2626 |
www.bigedsbbq.com

Sports fans and BBQ lovers "pig out" on the "down-home" eats at this "messy", "busy" Matawan 'cue shack, beloved for its "bargain" all-you-can-eat ribs (which are either "delicious" or "run-of-the-mill", depending on who's talking); "outdated" Western-themed furnishings and "sticky" housekeeping come with the territory.

Bistro at Red Bank *Eclectic*
| 21 | 19 | 20 | $39 |

Red Bank | 14 Broad St. (bet. Front & Mechanic Sts.) | 732-530-5553 |
www.thebistroatredbank.com

There's "something for everyone" at this Red Bank "fixture" featuring everything from pizza to sushi on its "interesting" Eclectic menu (regulars recommend its "legendary" crackling calamari salad); other assets include "helpful" personnel, a "cozy" setting and "fun" people-watching from sidewalk seats; P.S. NJ wines are on offer, but they "don't mind if you BYO."

Bistro Olé ☑ *Portuguese/Spanish*
| 23 | 19 | 22 | $40 |

Asbury Park | 230 Main St. (Mattison Ave.) | 732-897-0048 |
www.bistroole.com

Pucker up for "kisses" from "outrageous" owner Rico Rivera at this "splashy" Iberian BYO in Asbury Park, known for its "ample portions" of "captivating" seafood and paella as well as "amazing sangria" made from the wine you bring along; some say the place is "not what it used to be", yet there are always "long lines" on summer weekends – primarily due to the "no-reservations" rule.

		FOOD	DECOR	SERVICE	COST

❷ Black Duck on Sunset *Eclectic* — 26 | 22 | 24 | $47

West Cape May | 1 Sunset Blvd. (B'way) | 609-898-0100 |
www.blackduckonsunset.com

"First-class" cooking draws diners to this "out-of-the-way" Eclectic
in West Cape May, where regulars recommend you "definitely have
the duck"; "efficient" service, a money-saving BYO policy and a
"laid-back" setting in an "old Victorian" house add to its appeal.

Black-Eyed Susans Café ⓜ⇱ *American* — – | – | – | E

Harvey Cedars | 7801 Long Beach Blvd. (78th St.) | 609-494-4990 |
www.blackeyedsusanscafe.com

By day a coffeehouse, this seasonal, cash-only BYO in Harvey
Cedars morphs into a fine-dining destination after dark with the ad-
dition of white linens and candlelight; the farm-to-table modern
American menu comes via husband-and-wife team Christopher
Sanchez and Ashley Pellagrino, popular LBI chefs and caterers.

Black Trumpet *American* — 24 | 22 | 23 | $52

Spring Lake | Grand Victorian Hotel | 1505 Ocean Ave.
(bet. Madison & Newark Aves.) | 732-449-4700 |
www.theblacktrumpet.com

Recently transplanted to Spring Lake's oceanfront Grand Victorian
Hotel, this "true-find" New American purveys a "superb" menu of
"creative" selections, served in a "lovely" dining room or "splendid"
porch; a BYO policy and "unobtrusive", fit-for-"royalty" service
make the "upmarket" tabs easier to digest.

Blue Pig Tavern *American* — 21 | 20 | 20 | $42

Cape May | Congress Hall Hotel | 251 Beach Ave. (bet. Congress &
Perry Sts.) | 609-884-8421 | www.congresshall.com

"Delicious" breakfasts and breezy patio seating are among the "best
features" of this "quaint" tavern nestled inside Cape May's "his-
toric" Congress Hall Hotel; "terrific" Traditional American eats and
"old seaside" decor distract from the "no-bargain" pricing.

Bobby Chez ⓜ *Seafood* — 24 | 11 | 18 | $23

Margate | 8007 Ventnor Ave. (Gladstone Ave.) | 609-487-1922

(continued)

(continued)

Bobby Chez

Mays Landing | Shoppes at English Creek | 6041 Black Horse Pike (Cape May Ave.) | 609-646-4555
www.bobbychezcrabcakes.com

Famed for its "can't-be-beat" crab cakes (not to mention "rockin'" rotisserie chicken and lobster mashed potatoes), this "minimally decorated" duo in Margate and Mays Landing is mainly for "take-out" given its "no-atmosphere" settings; P.S. the food arrives partially cooked accompanied by an "idiot-proof guide" on how to reheat the grub "in your own oven."

Bobby Flay Steak Ⓜ *Steak*   25 | 25 | 24 | $65

Atlantic City | Borgata Hotel, Casino & Spa | 1 Borgata Way (Huron Ave.) | 609-317-1000 | www.bobbyflaysteak.com

Bobby Flay, the "god of grilling", proves that he "sure knows how to grill a steak" at this "outstanding" chop shop set inside Atlantic City's Borgata Hotel; a "superb" wine list and a "lavishly decorated" setting by David Rockwell embellish the overall "luscious" feel, but don't forget to bring all your credit cards – this one's priced for "high rollers."

Bobby's Burger Palace *Burgers*   21 | 15 | 17 | $17

Eatontown | Monmouth Mall | 180 Rte. 35 (Wyckoff Rd.) | 732-544-0200 | www.bobbysburgerpalace.com

"Very good" – "not outstanding" – hamburgers are upstaged by "killer" sweet potato fries and "sinful" shakes at this fast-food chain link in Eatontown from top toque Bobby Flay; the "retro-diner" setting may be too "stark" for some, but the "crunchified" burgers (with potato chips atop the patties) are "a must."

Bonefish Grill *Seafood*   21 | 19 | 20 | $35

Egg Harbor Township | 3121 Fire Rd. (Tilton Rd.) | 609-646-2828
NEW **Red Bank** | 447 Rte. 35 (Navesink River Rd.) | 732-530-4284
Brick | 179 Van Zile Rd. (Rte. 70) | 732-785-2725
www.bonefishgrill.com

The majority have "no bones" to pick with this "midlevel" Outback offshoot and "forget it's a chain", thanks to "fresh" fin fare and "friendly" service (management "clearly sends" the staff to "Server U") in "warm" environs; though some report "crowded", "chaotic" scenes on weekends, for most it remains a solid option "without going broke" for nights you "don't feel like cooking."

Brandl ☒ *American*   24 | 18 | 20 | $49

Belmar | 703 Belmar Plaza (bet. 8th & 9th Aves.) | 732-280-7501 | www.brandlrestaurant.com

Chef Chris Brandl demonstrates his "enormous skill" at this "unpretentious" New American BYO "hidden" in a Shore strip mall; true, it's "somewhat pricey for Belmar" and the "downscale" decor and "not-that-great" service "could be better", yet most feel this "little gem" has "special occasion" written all over it.

NEW Breakfast Room ☒☒ *American*   - | - | - | M

Atlantic City | Revel | 500 Boardwalk (Metropolitan Ave.) | 855-348-0500 | www.revelresorts.com

Atlantic City high rollers can ante up for a full American breakfast or grab-and-go options such as pastries from renowned chef Michel Richard at his midpriced AM-only spot at Revel; expect his signature whimsical touch in everything from French toast crème brûlée to filet mignon.

Brennen's Steakhouse *Steak*   23 | 20 | 21 | $48

Neptune City | 62 W. Sylvania Ave. (Merritt Ave.) | 732-774-5040

"Early-bird deals" are part of the "fantastic value" that's the lure at this "on-the-money" Neptune chophouse, where the "basic" menu aspires to "NY quality"; "cordial" employees and live piano music "make for a good time", though the "healthy bar scene" adds some "noise" to the otherwise "comfortable" surroundings.

Brickwall Tavern ☾ *Pub Food*   18 | 17 | 18 | $26

Asbury Park | 522 Cookman Ave. (Bangs Ave.) | 732-774-1264 | www.brickwalltavern.com

"Fun" times trump the "better-than-average" American pub grub on offer at this "noisy" Asbury Park "staple" that's probably more "sports bar" than restaurant; still, fans say the "easygoing"

| | FOOD | DECOR | SERVICE | COST |

atmosphere, "inexpensive" tabs and "live music" make it a "great place to chill."

Buddakan *Asian*
26 | 27 | 23 | $53

Atlantic City | Pier Shops at Caesars | 1 Atlantic Ocean (Arkansas Ave.) | 609-674-0100 | www.buddakanac.com

Stephen Starr's "phenomenal" Pan-Asian "scene" in AC's Pier at Caesars (a spin-off of the Philly and Manhattan outposts) offers "beautifully realized" fusion specialties in an "over-the-top" setting complete with a "giant" gilded Buddha and "glorious" communal table; ok, it's "very pricey" and "very noisy", but all agree that it's a "true experience" and "excellent for a special occasion."

Cafe Loren Ⓜ *American*
▽ 25 | 18 | 24 | $52

Avalon | 2288 Dune Dr. (23rd St.) | 609-967-8228 | www.cafeloren.com

This "upscale" Avalon BYO has been an "excellent" option for 30-plus years thanks to its "fabulous" American cooking and "lovely" service; despite "nondescript" decor and "pricey" tabs, devotees say it's an "excellent" alternative to the "crowded Cape May dining" scene.

Capriccio Ⓜ *Italian*
25 | 26 | 26 | $61

Atlantic City | Resorts Atlantic City Casino & Hotel | 1133 Boardwalk (North Carolina Ave.) | 609-340-6789 | www.resortsac.com

Diners "hit the jackpot" at this "outstanding" Italian in AC's Resorts Casino, where the winnings include "skillfully prepared", "osso good" dishes served by a "wonderful" team in a "stunning", "Gilded Age" setting replete with "fantastic" ocean views; but a post-Survey change in the hotel's ownership puts its ratings (and future) in question.

Capt'n Ed's Place *Seafood/Steak*
20 | 15 | 19 | $32

Point Pleasant | 1001 Arnold Ave. (Pine Bluff Ave.) | 732-892-4121 | www.captnedsplace.com

This "fun" BYO surf 'n' turf "haunt" down the Shore in Point Pleasant is best known for an "amusing" gimmick: "grilling your own" meats on a sizzling stone; small fry enjoy the tanks stocked with local fish – and their own menu – though grown-ups cite "long weekend waits."

	FOOD	DECOR	SERVICE	COST

Carmine's *Italian*

| 21 | 20 | 20 | $41 |

Atlantic City | Quarter at the Tropicana | 2801 Pacific Ave. (Iowa Ave.) | 609-572-9300 | www.carminesnyc.com

"Best with a group", this "noisy" AC spin-off of the NYC original is known for "heavy-duty old-school" Italian chow served family-style on platters "humongous" enough to "feed the entire Soprano family"; sure, it's a "bit of a factory" and a "tourist trap", but it's a good place to "let your hair down" and priced fairly.

Casa Solar ⓜ *Pan-Latin*

| 23 | 18 | 19 | $39 |

Belmar | 1104 Main St. (bet. 11th & 12th Aves.) | 732-556-1144

A "delicious" mix of "unique" Pan-Latin flavors is yours at this "unpretentious" Belmar BYO that's perfect for those "willing to try something that they're unable to pronounce correctly"; too bad it "suffers in the service department", but otherwise it's a "solid" bet.

Charley's Ocean Grill *American*

| 18 | 19 | 19 | $37 |

Long Branch | 29 Avenel Blvd. (Ocean Ave.) | 732-222-4499 | www.charleysoceangrill.com

Bermuda fish chowder is a menu "knockout" at this "steady" North Shore American, parked a block from the ocean in Long Branch; "friendly" bars upstairs and down feature "great" views (and multiple TVs), and though some find this old salt "better" since it was remodeled, critics contend "it's not what it used to be."

🆕 Chart House *Seafood*

| 21 | 26 | 21 | $53 |

Atlantic City | Golden Nugget Hotel & Casino | Brigantine Blvd. & Huron Ave. | 609-340-5030 | www.chart-house.com

"Well-prepared" surf 'n' turf and "attentive" service make this upscale chain seafooder housed in AC's Golden Nugget a "safe" bet, though some stern critics call it "average for the price."

ⓩ Chef Vola's ⓜ⇸ *Italian*

| 26 | 12 | 23 | $53 |

Atlantic City | 111 S. Albion Pl. (Pacific Ave.) | 609-345-2022 | www.chefvolas.com

"Difficult reservations" is putting it mildly at this "hidden" Italian BYO on an AC side street, where the "just-like-mama's" cooking enjoys a fervid "cult following" despite a cash-only policy, "low-ceilinged basement" setting and "tables closer than Siamese twins"; it's "no longer a secret" – "everybody knows the unlisted number" – and first-timers are willing to "sell their first-born" for a table.

Chelsea Prime *Steak* ▽ 24 | 27 | 23 | $65

Atlantic City | Chelsea Hotel | 111 S. Chelsea Ave., 5th fl. (Pacific Ave.) | 609-428-4545 | www.thechelsea-ac.com

Though the "A-plus" steaks are aged and the cocktails are "retro", the "crowd is 'now'" at this "beautiful" chop shop inside AC's boutique Chelsea Hotel; "lovely" service, "delicious" ocean views and sophisticated "black-and-white" decor right out of a 1940s "supper club" make the "expensive" tabs more understandable.

Chickie & Pete's Cafe *Pub Food* 17 | 17 | 17 | $24

NEW Wildwood | Boardwalk (Cedar Ave.) | 609-770-8833 ◐
Ocean City | Boardwalk (9th St.) | 609-545-8720 🅢 Ⓜ
Egg Harbor Township | 6055 Black Horse Pike (English Creek Ave.) | 609-272-1930 ◐
www.chickiesandpetes.com

"Loud and friendly", these "basic" South Jersey outposts of the Philly-based sports bar chain serve "typical" pub grub along with their "claim to fame": "addictive" crab fries (think french fries with Old Bay seasoning); although there are "TVs aplenty", service can be "hard to find."

Chilangos *Mexican* 21 | 15 | 19 | $27

Highlands | 272 Bay Ave. (bet. Marina Bay Ct. & Sea Drift Ave.) | 732-708-0505

"Above-average" Mexican chow washed down with "yummy" margaritas is the draw at this "small", no-reservations storefront in Monmouth County's Highlands; though some find the experience "hit-or-miss", there's nothing wrong with the "friendly" service.

Claude's *French* ▽ 27 | 22 | 26 | $51

North Wildwood | 100 Olde New Jersey Ave. (1st Ave.) | 609-522-0400 | www.claudesrestaurant.com

This "real surprise" ensconced in an "unlikely" North Wildwood address serves "fantastic" French bistro classics that transport Francophiles "back to St. Germain"; service that makes you "feel like family" pairs well with the "warm", "romantic" atmosphere; P.S. closed from October to mid-April.

Clementine's Café ⊠ *Creole* | 23 | 21 | 22 | $44 |

Avon-by-the-Sea | 306 Main St. (Lincoln Ave.) | 732-988-7979 | www.clementinesavon.com

"Think N'Awlins" and its "big" Creole flavors to get the gist of this "unique" little Avon BYO that's "like nothing else at the Shore" (for one thing, it's "one of the few to take reservations"); it's "decorated to the nines" with "kitschy" "knickknacks", although what's "colorful" for some is too "gaudy" for others.

Continental *Eclectic* | 23 | 23 | 21 | $38 |

Atlantic City | Pier Shops at Caesars | 1 Atlantic Ocean (Arkansas Ave.) | 609-674-8300 | www.continentalac.com

Stephen Starr's "cool" Eclectic offers a "seriously good", globe-trotting small-plates menu (and "even better cocktails") delivered by a "young, enthusiastic" team; the sprawling, "retro-chic" setting in Atlantic City's Pier at Caesars trumps the Philadelphia original with "amazing" "midcentury modern decor" and really "great ocean views."

Copper Canyon *Southwestern* | 23 | 21 | 18 | $47 |

Atlantic Highlands | Blue Bay Inn | 51 First Ave. (bet. Center Ave. & Ocean Blvd.) | 732-291-8444 | www.thecoppercanyon.com

"Delicious" Southwestern chow is the calling card of this "pretty" spot inside Atlantic Highlands' Blue Bay Inn, where the fare can be paired with "smokin'" margaritas concocted from a deep tequila list; "noisy" sound levels and "unfriendly", "rush-you-out" service are downsides, but otherwise the dining here is "first-rate."

Copper Fish *American/Seafood* | ▽ 20 | 21 | 19 | $48 |

West Cape May | 416 Broadway (bet. Congress St. & Sunset Blvd.) | 609-898-1555

The "chef knows what he's doing" at this American seafooder that relocated to the site of the former Daniel's on Broadway in West Cape May; though critics complain of "overpricing", "underportioning" and "disorganized" service, loyalists insist "it has potential";

P.S. there are a limited number of NJ wines on offer, but they're happy to have you BYO.

Crab's Claw Inn *Seafood*

| 18 | 15 | 18 | $36 |

Lavallette | 601 Grand Central Ave. (President Ave.) | 732-793-4447 | www.thecrabsclaw.com

"Basic" Shore seafood is dished out at this "relaxed" Lavallette "standby" known for "good-not-great" eats accompanied by "plenty of draft beer"; in the winter, it's a "destination for the retired crowd", but in season, "plan on a wait" – even though some say it's "past its prime."

Crab Trap *Seafood*

| 21 | 17 | 19 | $37 |

Somers Point | 2 Broadway (Somers Point Circle) | 609-927-7377 | www.thecrabtrap.com

"Old-school" fin fare arrives in a "classic" fish-shack setting at this "been-there-forever" seafooder in Somers Point that's a "senior hangout" off season and a "tourist" magnet come summertime; critics crab it could stand "a little updating" in the decor and service departments, but concede that the bar overlooking Great Egg Harbor is its "saving grace."

Crown Palace *Chinese*

| 20 | 19 | 18 | $29 |

Middletown | 1283 Rte. 35 (Kings Hwy.) | 732-615-9888 | www.crownpalacerestaurant.com

Weekend brunches rolling out a "wide variety" of dim sum are the hook at this Middletown Chinese, though the everyday "cut-above" cooking keeps it "always busy"; a "spectacular" fish tank speaks to its "upscale" aspirations.

NEW Cubacan *Cuban*

| - | - | - | M |

Asbury Park | 800 Ocean Ave. (Asbury Ave.) | 732-774-3007 | www.cubacan.net

South Beach meets the Asbury Park boardwalk at this upscale Cuban serving small and large plates, backed by moderately priced Spanish and South American wines in an urban-chic setting featuring rosewood floors, mosaic tiles and billowy white curtains with wrought-iron valances; ocean views and live bands on weekends complete the picture.

	FOOD	DECOR	SERVICE	COST

Cuba Libre *Cuban*

| 21 | 24 | 21 | $42 |

Atlantic City | Quarter at the Tropicana | 2801 Pacific Ave. (Iowa Ave.) | 609-348-6700 | www.cubalibrerestaurant.com

It's Havana by way of "Hollywood" at this "novel" Cuban inside AC's Tropicana, where "excellent" chow and "hospitable" service take a backseat to the "loud, bustling" scene and over-the-top decor (that includes a Soviet missile replica); even though it's a link of a national chain, fans of "something different" can't get enough of its "Latin flair."

Cucina Rosa *Italian*

| 21 | 18 | 21 | $39 |

Cape May | Washington Street Mall | 301 Washington St. (Perry St.) | 609-898-9800 | www.cucinarosa.com

The aroma of "homemade red sauce" lures patrons into this "must-visit" Italian BYO "conveniently located" on Cape May's Washington Street Mall; "reasonable" tabs, "pleasant" service and a patio with excellent people-watching opportunities ice the cake.

Daddy O *American*

| 19 | 22 | 19 | $46 |

Long Beach Township | Daddy O Hotel | 4401 Long Beach Blvd. (44th St.) | 609-494-1300 | www.daddyohotel.com

"Glitzy" for Long Beach, this "sleek" American brings a "W Hotel" vibe to the Jersey Shore with its "retro" "'60s" design, "NYC-cool" following and "top-shelf" bar scene; it's a "nice departure from the flip-flop crowds", even though its "haute cafeteria" offerings are "not cheap."

D & L Barbecue Ⓜ *BBQ*

| ▽ 24 | 10 | 16 | $30 |

Bradley Beach | 714 Main St. (bet. Lareine & McCabe Aves.) | 732-776-7488 | www.dlbbq.com

Having relocated from one seaside community (Asbury Park) to another (Bradley Beach), this "no-frills" BYO still slings "lip-smackin'" BBQ and "first-rate" mac 'n' cheese in a "no-atmosphere" setting; overall, it's a "solid" effort, save for the "slow" service.

Daniel's Bistro Ⓜ *Continental*

| – | – | – | E |

Point Pleasant Beach | 115 Broadway (bet. Baltimore & Boston Aves.) | 732-899-5333

This BYO in Point Pleasant Beach plies a thoroughly modern Continental menu, with the surf options just as popular as the turf;

though the room can be loud, cognoscenti report the meals proceed at a leisurely pace.

Danny's ◐ *Steak* | 20 | 16 | 19 | $41 |

Red Bank | 11 Bridge Ave. (Front St.) | 732-741-6900 |
www.dannyssteakhouse.com

"Affable" owner Danny Murphy can often be found at this Red Bank "mainstay" that's been in business since '69, serving "reliable" steaks and seafood as well as some "excellent" sushi; though most agree there's "nothing out of the ordinary" going on here, it is "close to the theaters" and hosts a popular "neighborhood bar" scene.

Dauphin Grille *American* | ▽ 22 | 23 | 23 | $45 |

Asbury Park | Berkeley Hotel | 1401 Ocean Ave. (6th Ave.) |
732-774-3474 | www.dauphingrille.com

The latest "winner" from Shore restaurateur Marilyn Schlossbach (Labrador Lounge, Trinity & the Pope, etc.), this eatery in Asbury Park's restored Berkeley Hotel features an "interesting" American menu with European accents; "inspired service", a "fun atmosphere" and a "beautiful" setting are reasons why it won't stay "off the radar" for long.

David Burke Fromagerie Ⓜ *American* | 25 | 24 | 24 | $64 |

Rumson | 26 Ridge Rd. (Ave. of Two Rivers) | 732-842-8088 |
www.fromagerierestaurant.com

Star chef Burke "got his start" at this "upper-crust" Rumson classic and his "modernized" revamp since taking over features "lighter" American "fare with flair" (including his signature angry lobster and cheesecake lollipops); though the crowd's as "Waspy" as ever, now its "intimate" rooms are "brighter" and the pricing so "expensive" that "budget-conscious foodies" reserve the experience for a "special occasion" – or go for "Tuesday burger night."

Dish Ⓜ *American* | 25 | 16 | 20 | $42 |

Red Bank | 13 White St. (Broad St.) | 732-345-7070 |
www.dishredbank.com

"Unexpected twists" on American comfort food fill out the menu of this "delightful" BYO set in a "small" Red Bank storefront; an "efficient", "friendly" crew makes the "challenging" acoustics and "tight-squeeze" seating ("keep your elbows close") more bearable.

Diving Horse *Seafood*

	FOOD	DECOR	SERVICE	COST
	∇ 24	20	21	$50

Avalon | 2109 Dune Dr. (21st St.) | 609-368-5000 |
www.thedivinghorseavalon.com

Named for an early-20th-century boardwalk attraction, this seafood-focused Avalon BYO is a "great addition" to the Seven Mile Island "scene", especially since both the staff and the fin fare are "young" and "fresh"; the "charming", whitewashed-farmhouse setting also features breezy patio seating.

☑ Dock's Oyster House *Seafood*

	FOOD	DECOR	SERVICE	COST
	26	21	24	$52

Atlantic City | 2405 Atlantic Ave. (Georgia Ave.) | 609-345-0092 |
www.docksoysterhouse.com

A "throwback to the *Boardwalk Empire*" era of AC, this circa-1897 seafood "icon" still scores high for its "fabulous" fin fare served by an "outstanding" team in a "days-gone-by" setting; nightly piano music and a "good" wine list help distract from the "noisy" decibels and modern-day prices.

NEW Dos Caminos *Mexican*

	FOOD	DECOR	SERVICE	COST
	–	–	–	E

Atlantic City | Harrah's | 777 Harrah's Blvd. (Brigantine Blvd.) |
609-441-5747 | www.doscaminos.com

Steve Hanson's BR Guest group brings Mexican into the AC casino mix with this Harrah's outpost of the upscale Manhattan-based chain known for guac prepared tableside and standout margaritas; spectacular bay views and a cool contemporary design that includes leather walls are other draws.

☑ Drew's Bayshore Bistro Ⓜ *American*

	FOOD	DECOR	SERVICE	COST
	27	–	23	$42

Keyport | 28 E. Front St. (Division St.) | 732-739-9219 |
www.bayshorebistro.com

Admirers are "impressed" with the "remarkable" "craftsmanship" and "honest cooking" of chef Andrew Araneo at this Keyport American BYO that's renowned for its "heartfelt" Cajun-accented eats with a "New Orleans kick", served by a "congenial" staff; a 2011 relocation to larger, more upscale digs may help alleviate the "wait" to get in.

| | | FOOD | DECOR | SERVICE | COST |

☑ Ebbitt Room *American*

26 | 26 | 26 | $65

Cape May | Virginia Hotel | 25 Jackson St. (bet. Beach Ave. & Carpenter Ln.) | 609-884-5700 | www.virginiahotel.com

"Fine dining" doesn't get much better than this "real memory maker" in Cape May's Virginia Hotel, where "heavenly" modern Americana is ferried by an "attentive but not overbearing" staff in a "relaxed", "romantic" atmosphere; though it all "comes at a price", it takes the Shore experience "to the next level"; a 2011 renovation may not be reflected in the Decor score.

El Familiar *Colombian/Mexican*

- | - | - | M

Toms River | Stella Towne Ctr. | 1246 Rte. 166 (Hilltop Rd.) | 732-240-6613 | www.elfamiliar.com

There's no need to choose between tacos and arepas, because this modest Toms River BYO offers a menu of both Mexican and Colombian dishes; maybe it looks like "*abuelita's* living room" and the staff can get "caught up in the soccer match", but at least its "homemade" cooking is the "real" thing.

Eurasian Eatery Ⓜ *Eclectic*

23 | 14 | 21 | $25

Red Bank | 110 Monmouth St. (bet. Maple Ave. & Pearl St.) | 732-741-7071 | www.theeurasianeatery.com

Red Bank is the site of this "longtime", "family-run" BYO located near the Count Basie Theater, featuring a "something-for-everyone" selection of "delicious" Eclectic vittles that includes some "unconventional" vegetarian choices; though some feel the decor could stand an "update", there's nothing wrong with the "brisk, friendly" service.

Europa South Ⓜ *Portuguese/Spanish*

21 | 16 | 21 | $39

Point Pleasant Beach | 521 Arnold Ave. (Rte. 35) | 732-295-1500 | www.europasouth.com

"Still going strong", this Point Pleasant Beach Iberian "institution" dishes out some of the "best" paella around, washed down with "excellent" sangria poured by "warm" waiters; the "dark" interior may be getting "a little tired", but stalwarts insist it's "been around forever" for a reason.

Far East Taste *Chinese/Thai*
23 | 6 | 21 | $20

Eatontown | 19 Main St. (Broad St.) | 732-389-9866 |
www.fareasttaste.com

Both Chinese and Thai dishes are offered at this small, "off-the-
beaten-path" BYO in Eatontown, where the "low-budget" grub and
"prompt" service show remarkable "attention to detail"; the same
can't be said about the "nonexistent" decor, however, so insiders say
takeout is a "better option."

Fin ⓜ *Seafood*
▽ 25 | 25 | 22 | $68

Atlantic City | Tropicana Casino & Resort | 2831 Boardwalk (Iowa Ave.) |
800-345-8767 | www.tropicana.net

"Unbeatable ocean views" combine with an "expertly prepared"
menu at this seafooder tethered to AC's Tropicana Hotel; though the
fin fare's "fantastic", fans also plug its outdoor "boardwalk" seating
and indoor sea-glass color scheme; sure, it all comes at an "expensive" price, but a 50-under-$50 wine list helps reel in costs.

Five Guys *Burgers*
21 | 10 | 16 | $12

Brick | Habitat Plaza | 588 Rte. 70 (Cedar Bridge Ave.) |
732-262-4040

Toms River | Orchards at Dover | 1311 Rte. 37 W. (bet. Bimini Dr. &
St. Catherine Blvd.) | 732-349-3600
www.fiveguys.com

"Juicy, greasy" burgers with "all the trimmings" "blow away" the
competition at this chain with links in Brick and Toms River, a "pres-
idential favorite" that's also prized for its "farm-to-fryer" fries and
"free peanuts while you wait"; maybe some "don't get the hype", but
these "bare-bones" joints are "taking the world by storm."

Fornelletto ⓈⓂ *Italian*
24 | 24 | 23 | $54

Atlantic City | Borgata Hotel, Casino & Spa | 1 Borgata Way (Huron Ave.) |
609-317-1000 | www.theborgata.com

Chef Stephen Kalt assembles a "superb", "attractively presented"
modern Italian menu at this upscale-casual spot inside AC's Borgata
Hotel; the "charming wine-cellar" decor makes sense given the "extensive wine list", leaving "pricey" tabs and "noisy" acoustics as the
only sticking points.

	FOOD	DECOR	SERVICE	COST

☑ 410 Bank Street   *Caribbean/Creole*
26 | 21 | 24 | $54

Cape May | 410 Bank St. (bet. Broad & Lafayette Sts.) | 609-884-2127 | www.410bankstreet.com

The "creative" Caribbean-Creole cooking of chef Henry Sing Cheng served by a "cheery" team keeps this Cape May "classic" an "absolute favorite"; it's on the "expensive" side, seating is "tight" and the Victorian setting is "not special", but devotees declare it "feels like Key West and tastes like New Orleans"; P.S. reservations are "a must", and you can "bring your best bottle" or opt for the NJ wines offered.

Frescos   *Italian/Mediterranean*
22 | 20 | 23 | $47

Cape May | 412 Bank St. (bet. Broad & Lafayette Sts.) | 609-884-0366 | www.frescoscapemay.com

Reservations are a must at this seasonal Med-Italian in "pricey Cape May", which "never disappoints" given its "flavor-rich" food and "above-and-beyond" service; like sibling 410 Bank, it's set in a "great old" Victorian house and offers local wines, though it's ok to BYO.

Gables, The   *Eclectic*
24 | 26 | 22 | $57

Beach Haven | Gables Inn | 212 Centre St. (bet. Bay & Beach Aves.) | 609-492-3553 | www.gableslbi.com

A "charming" Victorian B&B is home to this "impressive" Eclectic in Beach Haven, known for its "gourmet" meals and "gorgeous front porch"; it's "expensive" (though you can BYO), but a "romantic" mood and "accommodating" service make for "tried-and-true" "fine dining."

Gaetano's   *Italian*
20 | 16 | 20 | $36

Red Bank | 10 Wallace St. (Broad St.) | 732-741-1321 | www.gaetanosredbank.com

"Satisfying meals" for a "satisfying price" are plated at this Red Bank Italian that offers both BYO and wines from NJ's Westfall Winery; an on-site market and "casual" vibe offset the "plain" digs.

Gallagher's Steak House   *Steak*
22 | 20 | 21 | $56

Atlantic City | Resorts Atlantic City Casino & Hotel | 1133 Boardwalk (North Carolina Ave.) | 609-340-6555 | www.gallaghersresorts.com

"All the favorites" from the "traditional" NY chophouse chain – i.e. "good-quality" beef in "plentiful portions" – turn up at this

	FOOD	DECOR	SERVICE	COST

knockoff in Resorts AC; sure, you'll need to "bring your wallet" and purists sigh merely "average", but it's a handy way to "blow your jackpot winnings."

☒ Girasole *Italian*

26 | 23 | 22 | $53

Atlantic City | Ocean Club Condos | 3108 Pacific Ave. (bet. Chelsea & Montpelier Aves.) | 609-345-5554 | www.girasoleac.com

Situated in a "nice spot" – a condo a block away from the Atlantic City boardwalk – this "superior" Italian boasts "refined", "old-fashioned" cooking served in a "cool", sunflower-themed setting festooned with "Versace decorations"; it feels as though it's "miles from the hustle and bustle of the casinos" and draws the "local 'in' crowd" unfazed by the "high prices" and service with "a little attitude."

Grenville, The Ⓜ *American*

17 | 22 | 20 | $45

Bay Head | Grenville Hotel | 345 Main Ave. (bet. Harris & Karge Sts.) | 732-892-3100 | www.thegrenville.com

"Charming" is the word for this "pretty place" inside an old Bay Head hotel with a "Victorian-Shore" feel and a "little-bit-of-heaven" veranda; too bad the "old-fashioned" Americana is only "fair", leaving many to say it "could be a gold mine, but really misses the mark."

Grimaldi's Pizza ⊅ *Pizza*

25 | 14 | 18 | $21

Highlands | 123 Bay Ave. (bet. North & Spring Sts.) | 732-291-1711 | www.grimaldis.com

"Twentysomethings on shoestring budgets" who don't feel like "schlepping to the Brooklyn original" tout this "old-school" pizzeria in Highlands for its "exceptional" pies; all right, it "doesn't sell slices" and the decor is "typical pizza parlor", but devotees insist it's the "best in NJ, hands down."

Harvey Cedars Shellfish Co. ⊅ *Seafood*

23 | 11 | 17 | $31

Beach Haven | 506 Centre St. (Pennsylvania Ave.) | 609-492-2459
Harvey Cedars | 7904 Long Beach Blvd. (79th St.) | 609-494-7112
www.harveycedarsshellfishco.com

Embodying the "LBI experience", these summer "fish shacks" turn out "basic", "extremely fresh" seafood in "wear-your-bathing-suit" settings; the menus and service differ slightly – Beach Haven is nicknamed the 'Clam Bar' and comes with a side of manager "attitude" – but both share BYO and cash-only policies.

Ikko *Japanese*   **25** | **19** | **26** | **$29**

Brick | Brick Plaza Mall | 107 Brick Plaza (bet. Cedar Bridge Ave. & Rte. 70) | 732-477-6077 | www.ikkosteakhouse.com

Everyone from sushi purists to finicky grandkids have a "fine time" at this "something-for-everybody" Japanese BYO in the Brick Plaza Mall; "entertaining" hibachi and sushi chefs whip up their "super-fresh" handiwork in a large, "pleasant" space, tended by "person-able", "extremely attentive" staffers.

☑ Il Mulino New York *Italian*   **27** | **23** | **24** | **$71**

Atlantic City | Trump Taj Mahal | 1000 Boardwalk (Virginia Ave.) | 609-449-6006 | www.ilmulino.com

For an "impeccable" Italian meal on a "big night out" in AC, it "doesn't get any better" than this Taj Mahal facsimile of the legendary NY original; expect "insanely good" classic cooking, "white-glove" service from a tuxedoed team and a "beautiful", traditionally appointed setting – but since it's a definite "splurge", "bring the credit card with no balance."

Inlet Café *Seafood*   **20** | **15** | **19** | **$36**

Highlands | 3 Cornwall St. (Shrewsbury Ave.) | 732-872-9764 | www.inletcafe.com

This second-generation seasonal seafooder, "right on the water" in Highlands, features "terrific" dockside views from its big outdoor deck overlooking Sandy Hook Bay; although it's a tad "pricey" for what it is, regulars say its "first-rate" fin fare and "fabulous summer atmosphere" are hard to beat.

Inn at Sugar Hill Ⓜ *American*   ▽ **18** | **23** | **21** | **$38**

Mays Landing | 5704 Mays Landing-Somers Point Rd. (River Rd.) | 609-625-2226 | www.innatsugarhill.com

Sweet indeed are the fireplace-equipped Victorian dining rooms at this "quiet" Mays Landing inn that also boasts "can't-be-beat" veranda views of the Great Egg Harbor River; though the kitchen's Traditional American fare may lack consistency, the service is "top-notch."

Irish Pub & Inn ◑⇱ *Pub Food*

18 | 16 | 18 | $22

Atlantic City | 164 St. James Pl. (bet. Boardwalk & Pacific Ave.) | 609-344-9063 | www.theirishpub.com

This 24/7 "slice of old Atlantic City" may have a monopoly on the "best-priced" food and beer in town, served in a "dark", "wood and memorabilia"–lined barroom; the "decent" grub has a decided Irish lilt and tastes even better "post-clubbing", but bring cash as it doesn't accept plastic.

It's Greek To Me *Greek*

18 | 13 | 17 | $25

Holmdel | 2128 Rte. 35 (Laurel Ave.) | 732-275-0036
Long Branch | Pier Vill. | 44 Centennial Dr. (Chelsea Ave.) | 732-571-0222
www.itsgreektome.com

Folks needing a "souvlaki fix" tout these "serviceable" Greek BYOs offering all the "basics" in "modest", "diner"-esque environs; purists find them merely "average", but "fast" service and "moderate" prices make the overall experience more palatable.

Izakaya *Japanese*

23 | 25 | 21 | $59

Atlantic City | Borgata Hotel, Casino & Spa | 1 Borgata Way (Huron Ave.) | 609-317-1000 | www.theborgata.com

This "loungey" "new wave" Japanese pub in AC's Borgata Hotel may resemble a "swank" nightclub but turns out an "innovative" menu from star chef Michael Schulson that runs the gamut from sushi and sashimi to robatayaki; the "striking" setting and "hip" crowd make the "minuscule" portions, "pricey" tabs and "loud" acoustics more palatable.

NEW JBJ Soul Kitchen Ⓜ⇱ *American*

– | – | – | I

Red Bank | 207 Monmouth St. (bet. Bridge & Shrewsbury Aves.) | 732-842-0900 | www.jbjsoulkitchen.org

'Hope is delicious' is the motto behind this Red Bank project of Jon Bon Jovi's Soul Foundation, where diners pay a cash-only donation ($10 is suggested) for a professionally prepared three-course seasonal American meal (no alcohol), or volunteer at the eatery if they can't; with no reservations taken and limited hours, there's often a wait for the 30 seats in the cool modern digs.

| | FOOD | DECOR | SERVICE | COST |

Jimmy's *Italian*
| | 23 | 14 | 22 | $43 |

Asbury Park | 1405 Asbury Ave. (Prospect Ave.) | 732-774-5051 |
www.jimmysitalianrestaurant.com

"Throwback" sums up the mood at this "time-machine" Italian in
Asbury Park, where the traditional "red-sauce" cooking, "old-
school" digs and "experienced" waiters are a match for the "Sinatra
on the wall" (and "in the air"); given its "dicey" location, the "valet
parking" is a plus.

Jose's *Mexican*
| | ▽ 23 | 7 | 18 | $16 |

Spring Lake Heights | 101 Rte. 71 (Jersey Ave.) | 732-974-8080
Ok, this strip-mall Mexican BYO in Spring Lake Heights may be
"tiny", but few mind given its "top-notch" cooking for "barely any
money at all"; still, "schlocky" decor and staffers who "speak little
English" lead insiders to opt for "takeout."

Juanito's *Mexican*
| | 23 | 17 | 20 | $26 |

Red Bank | 159 Monmouth St. (West St.) | 732-747-9118 |
www.juanitosredbank.com

There's almost "always a crowd" at this Mexican BYO in Red Bank
thanks to "tasty", "authentic" cooking served for a "value" price;
"cramped" seating and "no frills" in the decor department are over-
ruled by the "bountiful" portions and "friendly" staffers.

Kanji *Japanese*
| | 24 | 20 | 22 | $32 |

Tinton Falls | 980 Shrewsbury Ave. (Rte. 35) | 732-544-1600 |
www.kanjisteakhouse.com

"Fab" sushi and the "freshest" sashimi turn up at chef Roger Yang's
Japanese BYO in Tinton Falls that's also praised for its "modern design", treat-you-like-"family" service and the "sizzle and show" at
the hibachi grill; a convenient nearby liquor store offering "good
sake selections" ices the cake.

Kaya's Kitchen Ⓜ *Vegetarian*
| | ▽ 24 | 22 | 24 | $25 |

Belmar | 1000 Main St. (10th Ave.) | 732-280-1141 |
www.kayaskitchenbelmar.com

Since it relocated to more "upscale" quarters, this "healthy", "hip-
pie" Belmar BYO is still offering an "extensive", "unusual" menu of

vegan and vegetarian dishes so "delicious" that "even carnivores" are intrigued; "earnest" service and a "mellow vibe" keep its "tree-hugging" fan base satisfied.

Klein's *Seafood*

| 19 | 15 | 17 | $35 |

Belmar | 708 River Rd. (bet. 7th & 8th Aves.) | 732-681-1177 | www.kleinsfish.com

Aficionados say the "simple", "nicely prepared" fish at this Belmar seafood "institution" tastes best when sitting "outside on the deck" taking in the "salt air" and "watching the fishing boats go by"; a few feel the prices "jumped the shark" with the addition of a liquor license, but overall it stays "bustling" for a reason.

Konbu Ⓜ *Japanese*

| ▽ 26 | 13 | 20 | $32 |

Manalapan | Design Ctr. | 345 Rte. 9 S. (Center St.) | 732-462-6886

It's all about the "great" sushi at this "no-atmosphere" Manalapan BYO where the fish is "very fresh", albeit "a little more expensive" than the norm; still, the chefs are "constantly updating" the rolls, the cooked items are "excellent" and service is uniformly "friendly."

Labrador Lounge *Eclectic*

| 25 | 17 | 22 | $36 |

Normandy Beach | 3581 Rte. 35 N. (Peterson Ln.) | 732-830-5770 | www.kitschens.com

Brought to you by Shore restaurateuse Marilyn Schlossbach (Dauphin Grille, Langosta Lounge, etc.), this "laid-back" Normandy Beach eatery exudes a "cool vibe" and offers an Eclectic menu that's "diverse enough to satisfy all palates", served by a "surfer-dude" staff; BYO makes it "easy on the wallet", but bottles of wine can also be purchased on-site.

NEW La Fontana Coast *Italian*

| - | - | - | E |

Sea Isle City | 5000 Landis Ave. (50th St.) | 609-486-6088 | www.lafontanacoast.com

Housemade mozzarella, gnocchi and desserts are just part of the extensive menu at this seasonal upscale Italian just a block from the beach in Sea Isle City; BYO and enjoy water views, plus sunny decor and an outdoor patio that evoke a seaside Italian villa.

	FOOD	DECOR	SERVICE	COST

Laila's ⊠Ⓜ *Caribbean* ▽ 22 | 15 | 20 | $38

Asbury Park | 808 Fifth Ave. (Main St.) | 732-988-8806 |
www.lailaslatin.com

"Like eating at a relative's house", this "small" Asbury Park BYO is
infused with "love", starting with its "full-of-flavor" Caribbean home
cooking; some contend the prices are "not in line" with the "storefront" setting, though the "happy" atmosphere is fine as is.

Langosta Lounge *Eclectic* 22 | 21 | 20 | $38

Asbury Park | Asbury Park Boardwalk | 1000 Ocean Ave. (2nd Ave.) |
732-455-3275 | www.kitschens.com

Another Asbury Park hit from Marilyn Schlossbach (Pop's Garage,
etc.), this "busy" boardwalk spot features her signature "vacation
cuisine", an Eclectic mix of "affordable" food items ferried by an "accommodating" crew; the atmosphere is "alive", and it's hard to beat
for "après-beach beverages" on the patio.

La Pastaria *Italian* 19 | 16 | 18 | $32

Red Bank | 30 Linden Pl. (Broad St.) | 732-224-8699 | www.lapastaria.com

"Consistent" is the word on this Italian trattoria in Red Bank where
the food is "solid", the mood "cozy" and the costs "reasonable"; sure,
it can be "crowded" and "cacophonous", but alfresco dining, "half portions" and "truly special specials" make this BYO a "local favorite."

La Spiaggia *Italian* 24 | 20 | 25 | $49

Ship Bottom | 357 W. Eighth St. (Barnegat Ave.) | 609-494-4343 |
www.laspiaggialbi.com

"Excellent all-around", this "popular" Northern Italian BYO via the
brothers Stragapede draws seasonal visitors to Ship Bottom on Long
Beach Island; "well-prepared" food and "way-cute" staffers divert
attention from decor that's "in need of an update."

L'assiette *American* ▽ 20 | 15 | 19 | $45
(fka Plate)

Surf City | 1403 Long Beach Blvd. (14th St.) | 609-361-7800 |
www.lassiettelbi.com

An "ambitious" New American menu with a "nod toward local sup-
pliers" is the bait at this "locavore" BYO in Surf City on LBI; the food

is "good" – "sometimes very good" – but the digs are "not very attractive" and it would benefit from a "more professional staff."

Lazy Dog Saloon *American* ▽ 23 | 21 | 24 | $40

Asbury Park | 716 Cookman Ave. (bet. Bond & Main Sts.) | 732-774-2200
"Down-to-earth" American fare comes as a "pleasant surprise" at this "intimate" hangout on Asbury Park's "Restaurant Row"; since it's all about the "service and the people" – "friendly" applies to both the staff and the patrons – this "casual" spot is "right on the mark", and there's a "great bar" scene to boot.

Le Fandy 🗷 Ⓜ *French* 25 | 18 | 23 | $54

Fair Haven | 609 River Rd. (Haute St.) | 732-530-3338
"Charming" Fair Haven is the site of this "sweet" French BYO where chef-owner Luke Peter Ong "knows his stuff", taking simple dishes and "making them special"; service is "caring" and the tabs "expensive", but what's "intimate" to some is just plain "cramped" to others.

Little Saigon ⊉ *Vietnamese* 25 | 10 | 20 | $26

Atlantic City | 2801 Arctic Ave. (Iowa Ave.) | 609-347-9119
"Authentic", "first-rate" Vietnamese cooking is the draw at this cash-only, off-the-boardwalk "find" in Atlantic City; granted, this small BYO has "no atmosphere" and is parked on an "uncharming street", but service is "friendly" and the price tags "relatively meager."

LoBianco 🗷 Ⓜ *American* – | – | – | M

Margate | 20 S. Douglas Ave. (bet. Atlantic & Ventnor Aves.) | 609-350-6493 | www.restaurantlobianco.com
From husband-and-wife team Nicholas and Stephanie LoBianco, this BYO New American bistro in Margate serves up a menu of moderately priced all-American faves such as short ribs, crab-cake sliders and fish 'n' chips in a bright, 'beach-casual' setting; hours vary by season, so call ahead or check the website.

Lobster House *Seafood* 20 | 17 | 18 | $40

Cape May | Fisherman's Wharf | 906 Schellengers Landing Rd. (Rte. 109) | 609-884-8296 | www.thelobsterhouse.com
This "quintessential" seafood experience–cum–"tourist trap" on Cape May's Fisherman's Wharf "never changes", providing "really

good", "right-off-the-boat" fin fare in a "big", "not-fancy" setting since 1922; given the "long waits" and "too-fast" service, insiders opt for the raw bar or "take-out window" for speedier dining.

Los Amigos *Mexican/Southwestern*

| 23 | 18 | 22 | $31 |

Atlantic City | 1926 Atlantic Ave. (bet. Michigan & Ohio Aves.) | 609-344-2293 | www.losamigosrest.com

This "long-standing" cantina in Atlantic City pairs "mouthwatering" Mexican-Southwestern chow with "great" margaritas; fans ignore the "so-so" decor and focus instead on the "festive" mood and "consistently good" service.

Lucky Bones
Backwater Grille ◑ *American*

| 20 | 16 | 18 | $32 |

Cape May | 1200 Rte. 109 S. (3rd Ave.) | 609-884-2663 | www.luckybonesgrille.com

"Made-from-scratch comfort food" that's "fairly priced" draws a "family" crowd to this "downscale" Cape May American, an "oasis of normal" amid a stretch of fine-dining establishments; it's revered for its "yummy" thin-crust pizza, not the "high noise level."

Luke Palladino *Italian*

| ∇ 26 | 18 | 23 | $49 |

NEW **Atlantic City** | Harrah's | 777 Harrah's Blvd. (Brigantine Blvd.) | 609-441-5576 | www.harrahsresort.com

Northfield | Plaza 9 Shopping Ctr. | 1333 New Rd. (Tilton Rd.) | 609-646-8189 | www.lukepalladino.com

Modern Italian "dining bliss" lands in Northfield via this storefront BYO from the eponymous chef, where the "beautifully prepared" seasonal menu emerges from an "open kitchen"; though the setting's so "tiny" that it's "hard to get a reservation", the early reactions are uniformly "ecstatic" here; the outpost in AC's Harrah's opened post-Survey.

Mad Batter *American*

| 23 | 19 | 21 | $33 |

Cape May | Carroll Villa Hotel | 19 Jackson St. (bet. Beach Ave. & Carpenter Ln.) | 609-884-5970 | www.madbatter.com

Renowned as a "great breakfast place", this "quaint" Cape May American also plies "prepared-to-perfection" lunches and dinners in a "homey" Victorian B&B (nothing beats "sitting on the veranda drinking something fun" here); still, fans say it's "worth a drive from anywhere" for its "classic eggs Benedict" alone.

Mahzu *Japanese* | 20 | 16 | 18 | $31 |

Aberdeen | Aberdeen Plaza | 1077 Rte. 34 (Lloyd Rd.) | 732-583-8985 | www.mahzu.net

This Aberdeen Japanese is a "safe" bet for "good", "plain-Jane" sushi or "fun" hibachi shows that appeal to small fry; the decor's "minimal" and the service "variable" (sometimes "slow", sometimes "too rushed"), yet this BYO is a "decent" option given its "reasonable" cost.

Matisse *American* | 22 | 23 | 22 | $49 |

Belmar | 1300 Ocean Ave. (13th Ave.) | 732-681-7680 | www.matissecatering.com

"Right on the beach", this "romantic" Belmar BYO boasts "stunning" ocean views that make the "exemplary", "well-prepared" American bill of fare taste even better; service is "knowledgeable" and the decor "bright and attractive", but some "wish it were more affordable."

McCormick & Schmick's *Seafood* | 20 | 19 | 19 | $43 |

Atlantic City | Harrah's | 777 Harrah's Blvd. (Brigantine Blvd.) | 609-441-5579 | www.mccormickandschmicks.com

An "enjoyable" choice for "business and pleasure", this "upscale" seafood chain link in AC's Harrah's offers a "daily changing" menu of "freshly caught" fare in an "upbeat" atmosphere; though it feels too "stamped-out-of-a-mold" for some, its "professional" service is a plus and the "happy-hour bar menu" lures the after-work crowd.

McLoone's *American* | 17 | 22 | 19 | $42 |

Asbury Park | 1200 Ocean Ave. (bet. 4th & 5th Aves.) | 732-774-1400
Long Branch | 1 Ocean Ave. (Seaview Ave.) | 732-923-1006
Sea Bright | 816 Ocean Ave. (Rumson Rd.) | 732-842-2894
www.mcloones.com

The casual vittles are "hit-or-miss" and "expensive for what you get" at this American trio from restaurateur Tim McLoone; still, "spectacular" water views at all three locations and "accommodating" service make for a "relaxed" dining experience.

	FOOD	DECOR	SERVICE	COST

Melting Pot *Fondue*
19 | 20 | 20 | $46

Atlantic City | 2112 Atlantic Ave. (Arkansas Ave.) |
609-441-1100
Red Bank | The Galleria | 2 Bridge Ave. (Front St.) |
732-219-0090
www.meltingpot.com

"It's all about sharing" and "cooking your own food" at this chain
with a "corporate heart", serving almost "every kind of fondue";
while it's a "romantic" "treat" for "younger couples" and "fun with a
group", critics contend it's "overpriced" for what it is; P.S. go with a
large party if you want "two burners."

Memphis Pig Out *BBQ*
19 | 13 | 17 | $29

Atlantic Highlands | 67 First Ave. (Center Ave.) | 732-291-5533 |
www.memphispigout.com

The "name says it all" at this "kitschy" "neighborhood" fixture in
Atlantic Highlands where "fall-off-the-bone-tasty" BBQ keeps cus-
tomers "pigging out"; the "well-worn" digs done up with an "unend-
ing display of pig paraphernalia" could sure use a "makeover", but
the "fun" mood and "cheap" tabs are fine as is.

Merion Inn *American*
24 | 22 | 24 | $44

Cape May | 106 Decatur St. (Columbia Ave.) | 609-884-8363 |
www.merioninn.com

This "refined" Cape May "tradition" may be done up in "charming"
Victorian style, but its "quite good" Traditional American cooking is
decidedly "21st century" and draws a "polo-shirt" and "driving-
mocs" crowd; "impeccable" service, nightly piano music and "hard-
to-beat" early-bird deals make this a "throwback in a positive way."

☑ Mia ⧄Ⓜ *Italian*
26 | 25 | 24 | $57

Atlantic City | Caesars on the Boardwalk | 2100 Pacific Ave.
(Arkansas Ave.) | 609-441-2345 | www.miaac.com

An "amazing", "Roman temple–style" space just off the lobby of
Caesars in Atlantic City is the site of this "classy" Italian "getaway"
via Georges Perrier and Chris Scarduzio; patrons "feel like Zeus him-
self" as they dine on the "stellar" specialties, and though it's "quite
expensive", the prix fixe dinner specials are an "outstanding value."

Mill at Spring Lake Heights ⓜ *American*

21 | 24 | 22 | $43

Spring Lake Heights | 101 Old Mill Rd. (Ocean Rd.) | 732-449-1800 | www.themillnj.com

A lakeside location – with "beautiful" views of Old Mill Pond – and a "modern" interior supply the "superb" atmosphere at this Spring Lake Heights "classic"; "better-than-average" American cuisine, "nice" service and "terrific" fixed-price meals appeal to "mature diners" and "special-occasion" celebrants.

Mister C's Beach Bistro *Seafood*

18 | 18 | 19 | $43

Allenhurst | 1 Allen Ave. (Ocean Pl.) | 732-531-3665 | www.mistercsbeachbistro.com

It's easy to "get lost" in the "fabulous" view of the ocean from the bar of this Allenhurst seafood "standby" (it's so close to the water that "you feel like you're on a cruise ship"); otherwise, the "ok" food and service are "inconsistent", and the interior "could be updated."

Molly Pitcher Inn *American*

22 | 25 | 23 | $48

Red Bank | Molly Pitcher Inn | 88 Riverside Ave. (Front St.) | 732-747-2500 | www.themollypitcher.com

Everything about this "old-world" Red Bank "grande dame" is "so civilized", from its "top-drawer" service and "going-back-in-time" ambiance to its jackets-required-at-dinner rule (Fridays and Saturdays); the "surprisingly good" Traditional American fare may be "on the expensive side", but few mind given the "gorgeous setting" overlooking the Navesink River.

Moonstruck ⓜ *American/Mediterranean*

25 | 25 | 25 | $51

Asbury Park | 517 Lake Ave. (bet. Main St. & Ocean Ave.) | 732-988-0123 | www.moonstrucknj.com

Folks are "awestruck" by the "magical atmosphere" at this three-story Victorian house overlooking Wesley Lake in Asbury Park, where a "top-flight" American-Mediterranean menu paired with "excellent" wines is served by an "exemplary" crew; it doesn't take reservations, but the "wait is worth it" – especially in the "cool" ground-floor piano bar.

	FOOD	DECOR	SERVICE	COST

Morton's The Steakhouse *Steak*
| 25 | 23 | 25 | $67 |

Atlantic City | Caesars on the Boardwalk | 2100 Pacific Ave. (Arkansas Ave.) | 609-449-1044 | www.mortons.com

A steakhouse "standard-bearer", this "big-ticket" chain link in AC's Caesars offers "excellently prepared" cuts of beef and "grand sides" "served professionally" amid an "ambiance of wealth and class"; some find it a bit "staid" and wish they'd "lose the raw-meat presentation" and "high" wine pricing, but overall it's considered "one of the best."

Mud City Crab House *Seafood*
| 24 | 14 | 19 | $33 |

Manahawkin | 1185 E. Bay Ave. (bet. Heron St. & Marsha Dr.) | 609-978-3660 | www.mudcitycrabhouse.com

This seasonal Manahawkin crab "heaven" (on the mainland just minutes from LBI) is a "best-restaurant-in-a-swamp" contender thanks to some of the most "awesome" crab cakes "this side of Baltimore"; though the setting's strictly "hole-in-the-wall", the service is "good" and the tabs reasonable; P.S. it doesn't take rezzies, so brace yourself for "exhausting" waits.

NEW Mussel Bar by Robert Wiedmaier ❷ *Belgian*
| - | - | - | M |

Atlantic City | Revel | 500 Boardwalk (Metropolitan Ave.) | 609-225-9851 | www.revelresorts.com

DC chef Robert Wiedmaier brings Belgium to Atlantic City with this gastropub at Revel; it features mussels and other Flemish faves like tarte flambé, as well as steaks, salads and cured meats, not to mention 150 beers and live rock 'n' roll in a tavern atmosphere that includes beer-bottle light fixtures and mussel shells embedded in the bar top.

Mustache Bill's Diner ⊟ *Diner*
| 24 | 15 | 21 | $16 |

Barnegat Light | Broadway & Eighth St. (Central Ave.) | 609-494-0155

Featured on the Food Network, this "quintessential" BYO diner in Barnegat Light on Long Beach Island is a "real"-deal kind of place where everything's made from scratch; the "hours are a little crazy" (call ahead), but regulars tout the "out-of-this-world" breakfasts; P.S. it accepts neither plastic nor reservations.

	FOOD	DECOR	SERVICE	COST

Nauvoo Grill Club *American* — 18 | 25 | 19 | $40

Fair Haven | 121 Fair Haven Rd. (River Rd.) | 732-747-8777 | www.nauvoogrillclub.com

Reminiscent of a "posh ski lodge", this "clubby" Fair Haven New American is set in a "lovely" "Arts and Crafts" space equipped with four fireplaces; since the menu is "average" and the service "inconsistent", regulars advise sticking with "simple preparations."

Navesink Fishery Ⓜ *Seafood* — 25 | 10 | 19 | $35

Navesink | A&P Shopping Ctr. | 1004 Rte. 36 S. (Valley Dr.) | 732-291-8017

"Easy to miss" in a Navesink shopping center, this "unpretentious" fish market-cum–BYO seafooder slings "simply prepared" fin fare that's "as fresh as it comes"; fans don't mind the "slow" service and "forget-about-it" decor – it's "all about the food" here.

Neelam Ⓜ *Indian* — 20 | 13 | 18 | $25

Middletown | Village Mall | 1178 Rte. 35 S. (New Monmouth Rd.) | 732-671-8900 | www.neelamrestaurant.com

A "standard" sampling of Indian chow that's "just plain good" turns up at this "unassuming" BYO; the lunch buffets are such "good value" that it's easy to overlook the "slow" staffers and "tired" decor.

Ⓩ Nicholas Ⓜ *American* — 29 | 27 | 28 | $84

Red Bank | 160 Rte. 35 S. (bet. Navesink River Rd. & Pine St.) | 732-345-9977 | www.restaurantnicholas.com

"Hot off its 10th-year anniversary", Nicholas and Melissa Harary's "fine-tuned" "crown jewel" in Red Bank is again voted the Shore's No. 1 for Food; look for "showstopping", prix fixe–only New American meals served by an "impeccable" team in an "understatedly elegant", jackets-suggested setting; it's a "flawless" experience that's "worth every hundred you spend", though insiders report you can dine for less (and à la carte) at the "hip", "more relaxed" bar.

Nobi *Japanese* — ▽ 26 | 17 | 22 | $30

Toms River | T.J. Maxx Plaza | 1338 Hooper Ave. (Bey Lea Rd.) | 732-244-7888

"Well-prepared" sushi made "true to form" from "always fresh" fish is yours at this modest Japanese BYO, a "best-kept secret" in Toms

River even though it's been around since 1997; "nice" sushi chefs and servers who "treat you like family" enhance the "cozy" mood.

NEW O Bistro & Wine Bar ◑ *American* — | — | — | M

Atlantic City | Revel | 500 Boardwalk (Metropolitan Ave.) | 855-348-0500 | www.revelresorts.com

Take in ocean views, sip cocktails and wines and share stylish plates both small and large from top toque Michel Richard (Central Michel Richard in DC), who brings his signature New American fare with a French touch to this circular poolside bar at AC's Revel; the calypso vibe suits his playful takes on specialty burgers, fish tacos, skate meunière and the like.

NEW Ohana Grill *Hawaiian/Seafood* — | — | — | M

Lavallette | 65 Grand Central Ave. (Bryn Mawr Ave.) | 732-830-4040 | www.theohanagrill.com

This cheerful Lavallette Eclectic (whose name is Hawaiian for 'extended family') offers an alternative to the usual seaside fare with creative Asian- and island-inspired surf 'n' turf; BYO means no boisterous bar crowds to disrupt the soothing setting, and there's a liquor store across the street; limited hours in the off-season.

❷ Old Homestead 𝖘 *Steak* 27 | 25 | 26 | $72

Atlantic City | Borgata Hotel, Casino & Spa | 1 Borgata Way (Huron Ave.) | 609-317-1000 | www.theoldhomesteadsteakhouse.com

"Killer" steaks are "cooked to perfection" at this "cavernous" spin-off of the NYC original occupying a double-decker setting in AC's Borgata Hotel; "typical leather" decor and "prompt, unobtrusive" service come with the territory, and don't forget to bring "deep pockets" to settle the "outrageous" bill.

Old Man Rafferty's *American* 18 | 17 | 18 | $29

Asbury Park | Steinbach Bldg. | 541 Cookman Ave. (bet. Bangs & Mattison Aves.) | 732-774-1600 | www.oldmanraffertys.com

"Dependable as a Swiss watch", this "casual" Asbury Park American slings "routine" "upscale diner food" and "ab-fab" desserts for "small" sums; a "pleasant" setting and a "large" menu with "lotsa choices" please the "pickiest" eaters, the "sophomoric" service not so much.

NEW Pacific Grill *American*

–	–	–	E

Wildwood | 4801 Pacific Ave. (Taylor Ave.) | 609-523-2333 | www.pacificgrillwildwood.com

From the team behind Cape May's acclaimed Union Park, this upscale seasonal BYO in Wildwood showcases executive chef John Schatz's global-inspired contemporary American lineup; warm colors, palms and bamboo give the casually elegant space a Pacific island flair.

Palm, The *Steak*

25	21	23	$66

Atlantic City | Quarter at the Tropicana | 2801 Pacific Ave. (Iowa Ave.) | 609-344-7256 | www.thepalm.com

"Perfect" lobster, "superb" steaks and "hefty" cocktails are the signatures of this "bustling", "special-occasion" chophouse chain link in AC with a "dark men's-club" look; "old-school" service seals the deal, so while it's "not cheap", most conclude it's "worth it."

Pete & Elda's ● *Pizza*
(aka Carmen's Pizzeria)

22	10	18	$23

Neptune City | 96 Woodland Ave. (Rte. 35) | 732-774-6010 | www.peteandeldas.com

Since 1957, this Neptune City "throwback" pizzeria has been slinging "amazing" "paper-thin-crust" pies; sure, it's "old", "loud" and a "world-class joint", but the mood's "friendly" and there's a fun "bar crowd."

Peter Shields Inn *American*

26	27	26	$61

Cape May | 1301 Beach Ave. (Trenton Ave.) | 609-884-9090 | www.petershieldsinn.com

For "gracious dining" facing the ocean, it's hard to beat the "dreamlike" setting of this 1907 Georgian Revival mansion in Cape May, where "A-plus" Americana is offered in a "quiet", "romantic" milieu with plenty of "space between tables"; "efficient" service and a "perfect-getaway" vibe distract from the fact that this BYO is "not cheap"; the 2011 arrival of chef Carl Messick (ex Ebbitt Room) and a dining room redo may not be reflected in the Food and Decor scores, respectively.

	FOOD	DECOR	SERVICE	COST

P.F. Chang's China Bistro *Chinese*   20 | 21 | 19 | $34

Atlantic City | Quarter at the Tropicana | 2801 Pacific Ave. (Iowa Ave.) |
609-348-4600 | www.pfchangs.com

"Light, delicious", "Americanized" Chinese food keeps fans "coming
back" to this "upscale" chain link in AC; though some call it "ordinary" and "loud", the "consistent" service is a plus, ditto the "smart"
menu "catering to people with allergies" and other needs.

Phillips Seafood *Seafood*   20 | 20 | 20 | $41

Atlantic City | Pier Shops at Caesars | 1 Atlantic Ocean (Arkansas Ave.) |
609-348-2273 | www.phillipsseafood.com

Crab dishes are the menu "highlight" of this AC link in the crusta-
cean-centric Maryland chain, which also features a view of the
beach from its Pier Shops at Caesars setting; those who find "nothing exciting" going on say it "doesn't live up to the original", but ad-
mit it's still a "pleasant change" from the casino norm.

Piccola Italia Ⓜ *Italian*   26 | 23 | 24 | $49

Ocean Township | 837 W. Park Ave. (Rte. 35) | 732-493-3090 |
www.piccolaitalianj.com

"Sophisticated" Italian cooking via "superb" chef Brian Gualtieri
"wows" locals at this "hidden gem" in a "hard-to-find" Ocean
Township strip mall; an "extensive" wine list, "skilled" service and
an "attractive" setting make for "truly memorable" dining.

Piero's Ⓜ *Italian*   ▽ 22 | 20 | 22 | $46

Union Beach | 1411 Rte. 36 W. (Patterson Ave.) | 732-264-5222 |
www.pierosrestaurant.com

A "nice neighborhood place", this longtime Union Beach Italian offers "very good" cooking that "won't break the bank" in "homey" environs; while weekend "live music" ratchets up the "festive"
atmosphere, some find it slightly "cheesy."

Plan B Ⓜ *American*   24 | 20 | 22 | $36

Asbury Park | 705 Cookman Ave. (Bond St.) | 732-807-4710 |
www.restaurantplanbap.com

Asbury Park's "Restaurant Row" is home to this "small but mighty"
eatery offering "original" New American fare in an "arty", brick-

walled setting; "thoughtful" service and a "cool" vibe make it an "A-list" choice for "adult" locals, while the BYO policy helps keep costs in check; the post-Survey arrival of chef Evan Victor (ex Amanda's, Elements) may not be reflected in the Food score.

Plantation *American* | 18 | 20 | 18 | $41 |

Harvey Cedars | 7908 Long Beach Blvd. (80th St.) | 609-494-8191 | www.plantationrestaurant.com

There's always a "good bar crowd" at this "relaxing" spot on Long Beach Island's northern end, "one of the only places with a liquor license" in these parts; though the American chow can be "hit-or-miss" and the service "spotty", at least the decor is "pleasant" and it's "open year-round."

Pop's Garage *Mexican* | 22 | 16 | 20 | $21 |

Asbury Park | Asbury Park Boardwalk | 1000 Ocean Ave. (2nd Ave.) | 732-455-3275

NEW **Shrewsbury** | The Grove | 520 Broad St. (bet. Meadow Dr. & Monroe Ave.) | 732-530-7677

Normandy Beach | 560 Rte. 35 N. (7th Ave.) | 732-830-5700
www.popsgaragenj.com

These "fun", "come-as-you-are" taquerias via Marilyn Schlossbach dish out "fresh", "consistently good" Mexican chow in beachy, seasonal settings; "budget" pricing and "inexperienced" help come with the territory; the Shrewsbury branch opened post-Survey.

Portofino Ⓜ *Italian* | 24 | 17 | 20 | $45 |

Tinton Falls | 720 Tinton Ave. (Sycamore Ave.) | 732-542-6068 | www.portofino-ristorante.com

Tinton Falls is the port of call for this "quite good" Italian known for staffers with an "outstanding memory" – the "list of specials is endless and provided verbally"; even though the tabs skew "expensive" and the service can be "slow", most leave here "stuffed and happy."

Raimondo's *Italian* | 24 | 18 | 22 | $45 |

Ship Bottom | 1101 Long Beach Blvd. (11th St.) | 609-494-5391 | www.raimondoslbi.com

"Busy all summer" (when reservations are at a premium), this Ship Bottom BYO on Long Beach Island draws crowds with "robust" Italian dishes that are "beautifully prepared with the freshest ingredients"; enthusiasts say it's "best off-season" when it's quieter, though its "fabulous" "bargain" early-bird deals are enjoyable year-round.

Ram's Head Inn Ⓜ *American*
24 | 26 | 25 | $57

Galloway | 9 W. White Horse Pike (bet. Ash & Taylor Aves.) | 609-652-1700 | www.ramsheadinn.com

A "short trek" but light years away from AC, this "elegant" Galloway "class act" (and sibling of The Manor and Highlawn Pavilion) serves "exquisitely presented" Traditional Americana with "wonderful formality" in a jackets-suggested milieu; the "romantic", candlelit digs appeal to "older" folks who think it's "outstanding in all areas" – save for the "not-cheap" tabs – and particularly perfect at "Christmas."

Raven and the Peach *American*
24 | 25 | 23 | $61

Fair Haven | 740 River Rd. (Fair Haven Rd.) | 732-747-4666 | www.ravenandthepeach.net

"Pretty", "softly lit" decor "reminiscent of *Casablanca*" is on par with the "outstanding" New American food served at this "sophisticated" spot in Fair Haven; granted, it's "pricey", but "worth it" for a "special evening" out, and the "splendid" staff makes a "genuine effort to please."

Ray's Little Silver Seafood *Seafood*
21 | 10 | 17 | $35

Little Silver | Markham Place Plaza | 125 Markham Pl. (Prospect Ave.) | 732-758-8166

Admirers "stick to the basics" and order the "simple, fresh" fish at this "low-key" strip-mall seafooder in Little Silver; the decor "hasn't moved into the 21st century" yet and it takes no reservations, but BYO keeps costs down and service is "nice" if "slow."

Red *American*
21 | 22 | 20 | $47

Red Bank | 3 Broad St. (Front St.) | 732-741-3232 | www.rednj.com

The "sexiest place to eat" in Red Bank, this "hip" resto/lounge slings "great" cocktails and "solid" New Americana (including "not-bad sushi") in a "modern", "nightclub-chic" setting; ok, it can be "pricey" and "loud", but its "trendy" followers are too busy "people-watching" to notice.

	FOOD	DECOR	SERVICE	COST

Red's Lobster Pot *Seafood*

| 24 | 16 | 19 | $37 |

Point Pleasant Beach | 57 Inlet Dr. (B'way) | 732-295-6622 |
www.redslobsterpot.com

This "incredibly good" seasonal seafooder in Point Pleasant
Beach is comprised of two parts: a basic, "self-serve" deck on
the water where "you can watch the boats" come in, and a
"cramped" indoor "shack" with a more ambitious, "fresh-caught"
menu; either way, make sure to "get there early", since this BYO
doesn't take reservations.

Red Square *Eclectic*

| 21 | 26 | 22 | $60 |

Atlantic City | Quarter at the Tropicana | 2801 Pacific Ave. (Iowa Ave.) |
609-344-9100 | www.chinagrillmgt.com

Renowned for its "sub-zero" vodka vault, this "upscale" restaurant/
lounge in Atlantic City's Quarter at the Tropicana serves "creative", "expensive" Eclectic eats, but is probably most appreci-
ated for its "amazing" cocktails; its perestroika-themed, "red
velvet"-lined room includes "romantic" private booths that enhance
the "enjoyable" experience.

Remington's Ⓜ *American*

| 21 | 22 | 22 | $47 |

Manasquan | 142 Main St. (bet. Parker & Taylor Aves.) | 732-292-1300 |
www.remingtonsnj.com

Fans suggest this Manasquan New American could be the "closest
thing to a NYC restaurant on the Jersey Shore"; the "interesting"
seasonal menu is "nicely presented", and service is "attentive" at
this "classy" spot.

Renault Winery Gourmet Restaurant Ⓜ *American*

| 21 | 22 | 22 | $46 |

Egg Harbor | 72 N. Bremen Ave. (Moss Mill Rd.) | 609-965-2111 |
www.renaultwinery.com

NJ's oldest winery (now a "secluded" Egg Harbor resort with its own
inn) is the site of this "rustic" American offering an "escape from
everything modern and urban"; while the six-course, set-price New
American menu is "tasty" enough, the "so-so" wines are another
story; P.S. dinner served Friday–Sunday only.

	FOOD	DECOR	SERVICE	COST

Richard's ⊘ *Deli*
| 20 | 12 | 20 | $19 |

Long Branch | 155 Brighton Ave. (Sairs Ave.) | 732-870-9133 | www.richardsdeli.com

This "old-school" Long Branch deli presents a "large selection" of "consistent" noshes for "reasonable", cash-only sums; "worn" decor is trumped by "friendly", appropriately "intrusive" waitresses.

Roberto's Dolce Vita *Italian*
| 21 | 17 | 19 | $40 |

Beach Haven | 12907 Long Beach Blvd. (130th St.) | 609-492-1001

For "good" "home-cooked" food at "fair" prices, check out this "informal" Beach Haven Italian that's open year-round; the atmosphere may be very "'70s", but service is "friendly" and "BYO adds to the value."

Rod's Olde Irish Tavern *Pub Food*
| 18 | 15 | 19 | $30 |

Sea Girt | 507 Washington Blvd. (5th Ave.) | 732-449-2020 | www.rodstavern.com

Set on the "Irish Riviera" in Sea Girt, this "family-friendly" joint features a "decent", usual-suspects pub menu; maybe it's "loud at the bar" and the decor "needs a makeover", but there's nothing wrong with the "reasonable" tabs and "mammoth" portion sizes.

Rooney's Oceanfront *Seafood*
| 19 | 21 | 19 | $45 |

Long Branch | 100 Ocean Ave. N. (Cooper Ave.) | 732-870-1200 | www.rooneysocean.com

The "standard seafood" takes a backseat to the "breathtaking views" of "swaying palm trees" and the "roaring ocean" at this "happy" Long Branch "'in' place"; sure, service can be "spotty" and the chow's "pricey for the quality", but the "raw bar is a treat" and the "see-and-be-seen bar scene" is among the best in these parts.

Ruth's Chris Steak House *Steak*
| 25 | 22 | 24 | $63 |

Atlantic City | The Walk | 2020 Atlantic Ave. (bet. Arkansas & Michigan Aves.) | 609-344-5833 | www.ruthschris.com

Loyalists love the "sizzling platters" of "oh-so-good buttery steaks" at the AC link of the "top-quality" chophouse chain that comes through with "winning" sides too; offering "old-style service" in a "traditional" setting, it's "expensive" but "utterly reliable", especially when you're "entertaining friends and clients."

Sage ⊄ *Mediterranean* — 25 | 15 | 22 | $39

Ventnor | 5206 Atlantic Ave. (Weymouth Ave.) | 609-823-2110 |
www.sageventnor.com

"Outstanding" modern Mediterranean cuisine keeps this cash-only
Ventnor BYO booked "even on weekends in the off-season"; a "diverse", "thoughtfully prepared" menu and "knowledgeable" service
compensate for the "close" tables and "noisy" acoustics.

Sallee Tee's Grille *American/Eclectic* — 18 | 16 | 18 | $34

Monmouth Beach | Channel Club Marina | 33 West St. (Channel Dr.) |
732-870-8999 | www.salleeteesgrille.com

"Hidden" in a "hard-to-find" location in Monmouth Beach's Channel
Club Marina, this "congenial" spot serves NY-style deli items at
lunchtime, then shifts to an Eclectic, "something-for-everyone"
menu at the dinner hour; "inexpensive" tabs and a no-reservations
policy translate into "long lines."

Salt Creek Grille *American* — 19 | 22 | 20 | $43

Rumson | 4 Bingham Ave. (River Rd.) | 732-933-9272 |
www.saltcreekgrille.com

"Aspen ski lodge meets NJ" at this "beautiful" "Arts and Crafts"
American in Rumson, where the "above-average", meat-centric fare is
"tasty" if "not fancy"; a fire pit and "noisy" bar scene make a for
"jumping" "young scene", and fans say it's "crowded for good reason."

San Remo *Italian* — 22 | 15 | 22 | $40

Shrewsbury | 37 E. Newman Springs Rd. (Rte. 35) | 732-345-8200 |
www.sanremoitaliana.com

Maybe it "doesn't look like much from the road", but this "small"
Shrewsbury BYO supplies "reliable" chow from a menu that's all over
the Italian map and served by a staff that's "on top of everything."

Sawa *Japanese* — 23 | 20 | 20 | $39

Eatontown | 42 Rte. 36 (Rte. 35) | 732-544-8885
Long Branch | Pier Vill. | 68 Ocean Ave. (Centennial Dr.) | 732-229-0600
www.sawasteakhouse.com

"Impressive" sushi and "entertaining" hibachi grills keep the trade
brisk at this Japanese duo also touted for its "accommodating" ser-

	FOOD	DECOR	SERVICE	COST

vice; Pier Village's "fun" outdoor seating offers "great people-watching" opportunities and a "lively" bar scene, while Eatontown's "giant" aquariums thrill small fry.

Scarborough Fair Ⓜ American
23 | 25 | 21 | $42

Sea Girt | 1414 Meetinghouse Rd. (Rte. 35) | 732-223-6658 | www.scarboroughfairrestaurant.com

Private alcoves on many levels enhance the "cozy", "wonderfully romantic" mood at this atmospheric Sea Girt spot set in a 19th-century farm building; "cooked-to-perfection" New Americana served by a "professional" team make it perfect for "special occasions."

NEW Scarduzio's Ⓜ Japanese/Steak
- | - | - | VE

Atlantic City | Showboat Casino | 801 Boardwalk (bet. Delaware & States Aves.) | 609-343-4330 | www.showboatac.com

This high-end steakhouse/sushi lounge in the Showboat is celeb chef Chris Scarduzio's second AC property (after Mia, at Caesars); Wagyu and other prime cuts of beef from NYC's DeBragga butchers fuel high rollers in a big, modern setting featuring an open kitchen, sushi bar and late-night lounge with live entertainment.

SeaBlue Seafood
26 | 25 | 25 | $69

Atlantic City | Borgata Hotel, Casino & Spa | 1 Borgata Way (Huron Ave.) | 609-317-8220 | www.theborgata.com

Celeb chef Michael Mina's "seafood experience" just off the Borgata casino floor in AC is famed for its "decadent" signature lobster pot pie, served in a "picture-worthy" Adam Tihany–designed space (complete with "plasma screens doubling as fish tanks"); "stellar" service and a swanky mood make the "mortgage-payment" price tags "worth the splurge."

Shipwreck Grill American/Seafood
24 | 18 | 21 | $50

Brielle | 720 Ashley Ave. (Higgins Ave.) | 732-292-9380 | www.shipwreckgrill.com

"Always busy", this "unassuming" American seafooder in Brielle is a "consistent performer", with "top-notch" cooking and "exceptional" service; too bad the "way-too-loud" acoustics make for "sign-language" conversations, but overall it's a "nice local place."

	FOOD	DECOR	SERVICE	COST

Shipwreck Point *Steak*
- - - E

Point Pleasant Beach | 20 Inlet Dr. (B'way) | 732-899-3800 |
www.shipwreckpointsteakhouse.com

From the veterans behind Brielle's popular Shipwreck Grill comes
this Point Pleasant Beach chophouse where NYC-style dining comes
at NYC prices (i.e. most everything's à la carte); fortunately, the impressive wine list includes a good selection under $50.

Shogun *Japanese/Steak*
21 18 19 $36

Toms River | Bey Lea Golf Course | 1536 N. Bay Ave. (Oak Ave.) |
732-286-9888 | www.shogunbeylea.com

"Standard" hibachi shows keep the kiddies entertained at this
"Benihana-type" Toms River Japanese that also slices "pretty good"
sushi; it's a "fun" option and "great for celebrating birthdays", despite somewhat "sterile" decor and "rushed" service.

Siam Garden *Thai*
24 22 22 $33

Red Bank | The Galleria | 2 Bridge Ave. (Front St.) | 732-224-1233 |
www.siamgardenrestaurant.com

"As good as it gets" in Red Bank for Thai cooking, this "popular"
Siamese is also celebrated for its "beautiful" setting decorated with
an exotic mix of silks, antiques and woodcarvings; "genuinely warm
service" adds to the "pleasant experience", as does a location that's
"perfect for a pre-theater dinner."

Simon Prime Ⓜ *Steak*
- - - E

Atlantic City | Atlantic City Hilton | 3400 Pacific Ave. (Boston Ave.) |
609-347-7111 | www.hiltonac.com

'Rock 'n' roll chef' Kerry Simon lands inside AC's recently renovated
Hilton with this "slick" steakhouse where the servers wear jeans and
sneakers, and the tablecloth-free setting has a modern, sexy vibe;
just be prepared to "wield a black Amex card" when the bill arrives.

Sirena *Italian*
23 25 18 $52

Long Branch | Pier Vill. | 27 Ocean Ave. (Cooper Ave.) | 732-222-1119 |
www.sirenaristorante.com

This "beauty at the beach" in Long Branch's Pier Village offers
"delicious, beautifully presented" Italian food that tastes even

better when gazing out the "floor-to-ceiling windows" at its "standout" ocean views; maybe the staff "needs an attitude adjustment", but otherwise this "sophisticated" joint more than "lives up to its prices."

Smithville Inn *American*

20 | 22 | 22 | $40

Smithville | 1 N. New York Rd. (Old New York Rd.) | 609-652-7777 | www.smithvilleinn.com

"Quaint and quiet" sums up the scene at this "charming" "throwback" set in a 1787 Smithville building that more than "lives up to its history"; "respectable" Traditional American grub, a "laid-back" mood and "dependable" service all make for "nostalgic", "comfortable" dining.

Sofia *Mediterranean*

23 | 25 | 22 | $42

Margate | 9314 Amherst Ave. (Adams Ave.) | 609-822-9111 | www.sofiaofmargate.com

"Homemade" Mediterranean dishes are served at this "delightful" Margate venue where the "beautiful" setting (complete with four working fireplaces and a "wonderful" patio) is on par with the "delicious" food; grilled whole fish is the specialty of the house, and although it's on the pricey side, the "early-bird deal is a steal."

Sono Sushi *Japanese*

25 | 15 | 21 | $32

Middletown | Village Mall | 1098 Rte. 35 S. (New Monmouth Rd.) | 732-706-3588 | www.sonosushi.net

"High-quality fresh fish" fills out the menu of this "family-run" Japanese BYO in Middletown, an "old favorite" esteemed for its "satisfying", "interesting" sushi; "faithful" followers like the "nice" service but feel that the decor "needs a serious revamp."

Spargo's Grille Ⓜ *American*

23 | 17 | 21 | $41

Manalapan | Andee Plaza | 130 Rte. 33 W. (Millhurst Rd.) | 732-294-9921 | www.spargosgrille.com

A chef who's "not averse to experimenting" concocts an "outstanding" New American menu at this "unexpectedly good" Manalapan BYO parked in a "nondescript" shopping plaza; the prix fixe and early-bird options are "great bargains", and "excellent" service seals the deal.

Spike's *Seafood*

22 | 9 | 17 | $31

Point Pleasant Beach | 415 Broadway (Channel Dr.) | 732-295-9400

It's all about the "honest", "just-caught" fish at this Point Pleasant Beach fishmonger equipped with a "few tables" for dining; "dive" decor, "uncomfortable" bench seating and "eternal waits" (due to no reservations) come with the territory, but at least it's BYO.

Squan Tavern Ⓜ *Italian*

20 | 13 | 19 | $28

Manasquan | 15 Broad St. (Main St.) | 732-223-3324 | www.squantavern.com

"Everybody seems to know everybody" at this longtime Manasquan Southern Italian that's been serving an "old-fashioned red-sauce" menu and "scrumptious" pizza since '64; the "homey" atmosphere distracts from the "average" decor, no-rezzie rule and weekend waits.

Stella Marina *Italian*

23 | 23 | 20 | $46

Asbury Park | 800 Ocean Ave. (Asbury Ave.) | 732-775-7776 | www.stellamarinarestaurant.com

Another "slick" Shore Italian from the Cetrulo restaurant group, this "trendy" Asbury Parker offers "really good" food and a "well-priced" wine list in a "stunning boardwalk" setting boasting "picture-perfect views of the Atlantic"; "irregular" service and a "deafening din" are the downsides, yet many call it "outstanding all around."

Steve & Cookie's by the Bay *American*

25 | 22 | 23 | $52

Margate | 9700 Amherst Ave. (Monroe Ave.) | 609-823-1163 | www.steveandcookies.com

Known as a year-round Margate "mainstay", this "locavore heaven" near the AC casinos is also renowned for its "crazy good" seasonal New Americana as well as its "friendly" owner, Cookie Till; it's "*the* place to be seen" and "mobbed in summer", though retiring types "ask to be seated in the piano room where you're entertained."

Sumo *Japanese*

∇ 25 | 21 | 25 | $30

Wall | Allaire Plaza | 1933 Rte. 35 (Allaire Rd.) | 732-282-1388 | www.sumowalltwp.com

Sushi and hibachi fans rave about this under-the-radar Japanese set in a Wall shopping center, where "fresh" sushi and "really good" hibachi items are dispensed by a "smiling" crew; there are "lots of choices" on the menu, and thanks to the BYO policy, the price is right.

Surf Taco *Mexican* | 21 | 14 | 17 | $14 |

Belmar | 1003 Main St. (10th Ave.) | 732-681-3001
Long Branch | 94 Brighton Ave. (2nd Ave.) | 732-229-7873
Manasquan | 121 Parker Ave. (Stockton Lake Blvd.) | 732-223-7757
NEW **Red Bank** | 35 Broad St. (bet. Mechanic & White Sts.) | 732-936-1800
Forked River | 44 Manchester Ave. (Lacey Rd.) | 609-971-9996
Point Pleasant Beach | 1300 Richmond Ave. (Marcia Ave.) | 732-701-9000
Toms River | 1887 Hooper Ave. (bet. Church & Moore Rds.) | 732-255-3333
www.surftaco.com

Folks in the mood for a "quickie" tout this "popular" BYO counter-service chainlet for "cheap", "tasty" Mexican chow served in "no-ambiance", surfer-themed settings.

Taka Ⓜ *Japanese* | 25 | 25 | 24 | $41 |

Asbury Park | 632 Mattison Ave. (Main St.) | 732-775-1020 | www.takaapnj.com

Chef Taka Hirai's "Nuevo Japanese" in Asbury Park draws huzzahs for his "exceptional" sushi and "delicious" cooked fare; the "sophisticated" "Zen" setting is abetted by "great service" from an "easy-on-the-eyes" staff and, best of all, "BYO keeps tabs low."

Takara *Japanese* | ▽ 20 | 19 | 15 | $32 |

Oakhurst | Orchard Plaza | 1610 Rte. 35 S. (bet. Deal Rd. & Park Ave.) | 732-663-1899 | www.takarasteakhousenj.com

An "interesting mix of all things Asian" distinguishes this family-run Japanese in the Oakhurst section of Ocean Township; pricing is reasonable and the decor "unusually pleasant and peaceful", despite a full bar equipped with high-def TVs.

Teak *Asian* | 21 | 21 | 18 | $44 |

Red Bank | 64 Monmouth St. (Drummond Pl.) | 732-747-5775 | www.teakrestaurant.com

"Trendy" sums up this "hip" Asian near Red Bank's Theater District, where the "quality" menu takes a backseat to the happening vibe; regulars say it's "all about the bar scene", citing an "overpowering din" and "crazy-busy" weekends, while bargain-hunters sidestep the "high" tabs on "half-price Monday nights"; a post-Survey renovation may not be reflected in the Decor score.

Teplitzky's *Diner* ▽ 18 | 18 | 19 | $26

Atlantic City | Chelsea Hotel | 111 S. Chelsea Ave. (Pacific Ave.) | 609-428-4550 | www.thechelsea-ac.com

AC's "über-trendy" Chelsea Hotel houses this "kitschy" diner that's a "good getaway" from the casino bustle; service is "pleasant", the "retro" '50s setting "fun" and breakfasts may be "the best" choice on the "small, focused" menu.

Tim McLoone's Supper Club *American* 20 | 23 | 20 | $50

Asbury Park | 1200 Ocean Ave. (bet. 4th & 5th Aves.) | 732-774-1155 | www.timmcloonessupperclub.com

Imagine an "old-style" "NY supper club" to get the gist of this Asbury Park homage via the eponymous restaurateur, set on the boardwalk above McLoone's Asbury Grille; "oceanfront" views and a "great" floor show with "talented musicians" make the "decent but overpriced" New American fare taste even better.

Tisha's Fine Dining *American* 25 | 20 | 24 | $48

Cape May | Washington Street Mall | 322 Washington St. (Jackson St.) | 609-884-9119 | www.tishasfinedining.com

Now "open year-round" for breakfast, lunch and dinner, this Cape May New American BYO moved to larger digs in the Washington Street Mall in 2010 but still offers "excellent" grub and "attentive" service; though it "lacks the ocean view" of old and feels a bit more "sterile" than before, most report it's just as "fantastic" as ever.

Toast *American* 22 | 15 | 18 | $21

Asbury Park | 516 Cookman Ave. (bet. Bangs & Grand Aves.) | 732-776-5900 | www.toastasbury.com

This Asbury Park outpost of a popular Montclair breakfast-and-lunch specialist offers "tasty" American meals in a storefront space with doors that open on to the sidewalk as well as an outdoor patio; come "early", for this BYO doesn't take reservation.

		FOOD	DECOR	SERVICE	COST

Tomatoes *Californian/Eclectic* | 25 | 23 | 23 | $51 |

Margate | 9300 Amherst Ave. (Washington Ave.) | 609-822-7535 |
www.tomatoesmargate.com

There's "major bar activity" at this Cal-Eclectic in Margate, a "Shore favorite" where the "excellent" chow is a match for the "beautiful-people scene"; granted, it's "pricey" and can get "loud" during prime times, but it's a "no-brainer" for those in the mood for "lively" dining.

Tony Luke's ● *Cheesesteaks* | 20 | 11 | 16 | $16 |

Atlantic City | Borgata Hotel, Casino & Spa | 1 Borgata Way (Huron Ave.) |
609-317-1000 | www.theborgata.com
NEW **Wildwood** | 6200 New Jersey Ave. (bet. Sweetbriar &
Wisteria Rds.) | 609-770-7033 | www.tonylukes.com

"Not the same as eating on a Philly street corner" – but "just as messy" – this cheesesteak specialist in the food court section of AC's Borgata draws mixed responses: "can't beat it" vs. "close but no cigar"; all agree there's "no atmosphere", but it's not true "you can gain weight just looking at them"; the Wildwood sibling opened post-Survey.

Tony's Baltimore Grill ● *Pizza* | 18 | 8 | 16 | $20 |

Atlantic City | 2800 Atlantic Ave. (Iowa Ave.) | 609-345-5766 |
www.tonysbaltimoregrill.com

"Like stepping into an Edward Hopper painting", this AC pizzeria is a "cross between a dive bar and a cafeteria", with "stark lighting", "faded linoleum" and table-mounted jukeboxes; the "bar is open 24/7", and the "old-fashioned", "gum-chewing" waitresses add to the "blast-from-the-past" atmosphere.

Trinity Ⓜ *American* | 25 | 24 | 22 | $40 |

Keyport | 84 Broad St. (bet. Front & 3rd Sts.) | 732-888-1998 |
www.trinitykeyport.com

Appropriately "heavenly" cooking issues from the "ambitious" kitchen of this Keyport New American set in a "converted church" and praised for its "sinful", seasonal menu; the "magnificent" setting – complete with "soaring ceilings" and frosted-glass windows – is a match for the "outstanding" service, and there's "live entertainment" on weekends to boot.

	FOOD	DECOR	SERVICE	COST

Trinity & the Pope ⓜ *Cajun/Creole*

| 21 | 23 | 22 | $35 |

Asbury Park | 649 Mattison Ave. (Bond St.) | 732-807-3435 |
www.trinityandthepope.com

This "good-time" outpost of the Marilyn Schlossbach "empire" set
in a "beautiful" old Asbury Park bank puts a "sexy" spin on New
Orleans–style Cajun-Creole cooking in a "noisy" setting fueled by
"great" music and "very strong" drinks; a post-Survey renovation
may not be reflected in the Decor score.

Tun Tavern ⓓ *American*

| 18 | 17 | 17 | $32 |

Atlantic City | Sheraton Atlantic City | 2 Convention Blvd. (Baltic Ave.) |
609-347-7800 | www.tuntavern.com

"Beer is the star" of the show at this "casual" American microbrewery
set in the AC Sheraton "near the convention center"; though service
is "slow" and the chow's merely "acceptable", there are "lots of TVs"
for sports fans, the decor is "cool" and the mood is "fun."

Tuzzio's *Italian*

| 20 | 11 | 20 | $30 |

Long Branch | 224 Westwood Ave. (Morris Ave.) | 732-222-9614 |
www.tuzzios.com

"No fuss", "no pretense" and no reservations sum up the scene at
this "old-time" "neighborhood" Italian in Long Branch; though "decor isn't its strong point", locals like its "welcoming" service and
"family-oriented" approach, adding that the "reliable" cooking is
also a "good value."

Ugly Mug ⓓ *Pub Food*

| 15 | 14 | 16 | $25 |

Cape May | 426 Washington St. (Decatur St.) | 609-884-3459

"Simple is better" could be the motto of this way-"casual" American
pub in Cape May's Washington Street Mall, where the "average" grub
plays second fiddle to the "fun bar" scene; while it attracts a "younger
crowd" bent on "getting its drink on", some "old salts drift in" too.

Undici *Italian*

| 22 | 24 | 20 | $57 |

Rumson | 11 W. River Rd. (Bingham Ave.) | 732-842-3880 |
www.undicirestaurant.com

"Gorgeous" "Tuscan villa" design "transports you to Italy" at this
"sophisticated" Italian, a Rumson favorite famed for its "profoundly

authentic" cooking and "extensive" wine list; the "lively" bar can be "loud" and it's an "expensive endeavor", so "get someone else to pick up the check" – or else stick with the "great" appetizers and wood-fired pizza.

Union Park Dining Room *American*

| 25 | 24 | 24 | $55 |

Cape May | Hotel Macomber | 727 Beach Ave. (Howard St.) | 609-884-8811 | www.unionparkdiningroom.com

This "elegant" venue in Cape May's Hotel Macomber serves "innovative", "expertly prepared" New Americana in a "spacious" setting complete with a veranda sporting ocean views; it's the epitome of "classy", "memorable" dining – with "formal" service and appropriately "upscale" tabs – and although a BYO, it also serves local wines.

Ventura's Greenhouse ● *Italian*

| 18 | 16 | 17 | $34 |

Margate | 106 S. Benson Ave. (Atlantic Ave.) | 609-822-0140 | www.venturasgreenhouse.com

More "social experience" than fine-dining experience, this "enjoyable" Margate double-decker features a "basic" Italian menu upstairs and more "pub"-like chow on the ground floor, but is probably most memorable for its views of the ocean and seaside attraction Lucy the Elephant; you can always count on "lots of action" at the bar, however.

Vic's Ⓜ *Italian/Pizza*

| 21 | 12 | 19 | $24 |

Bradley Beach | 60 Main St. (Evergreen Ave.) | 732-774-8225 | www.vicspizza.com

Experience "bygone days at the Jersey Shore" at this fourth-generation family pizzeria in Bradley Beach, where regulars stick to the "addictive" thin-crust pies and "avoid the rest of the menu"; service can be "indifferent" and there's "no ambiance" in the "loud", "knotty pine"-lined room, but the tabs are really "cheap."

Villa Vittoria *Italian*

| 23 | 19 | 22 | $41 |

Brick | 2700 Hooper Ave. (Cedar Bridge Ave.) | 732-920-1550 | www.villavittoria.com

Look for a "big menu" of "old-fashioned" "red-sauce" standards at this "white-tablecloth" Italian in Brick that draws locals with its "uncompromising quality"; ok, maybe the decor is "a bit dated" and the crowd is from the "Sinatra" era, but genuinely "friendly" service makes for a "pleasant evening out."

Wasabi 34 *Japanese*

| 24 | 17 | 21 | $34 |

Matawan | 392 State Rte. 34 (Clover Hill Rd.) | 732-566-1888 | www.wasabi34.com

This Matawan Japanese features "wonderful" sushi, cooked items such as tempura and soba, and service "with a smile", but no sake (it's BYO) in basic surroundings.

☒ Washington Inn *American*

| 28 | 26 | 27 | $57 |

Cape May | 801 Washington St. (Jefferson St.) | 609-884-5697 | www.washingtoninn.com

Still the "gold standard" for "benchmark" fine dining in Cape May, this "classy" destination is all about "flawless attention to detail", from its "sensational", "artistically presented" Traditional American menu and "nice wine list" to the "gets-everything-right" service and "romantic" setting in a former plantation home; the "pricey" tabs notwithstanding, this one's a natural for "special occasions."

West Lake Seafood *Chinese*

| 25 | 12 | 19 | $29 |

Matawan | Pine Crest Plaza | 1016 Rte. 34 (Broad St.) | 732-290-2988 | www.westlakeseafood.com

Like "Chinatown in Matawan", this shopping-plaza BYO is known for its "fresh", right-"from-the-tank" seafood as well as "authentic" specialties "rarely served outside the big city"; too bad the decor and service "don't match the food", but it is "moderately priced" and there's "nice" dim sum on weekends.

What's Your Beef? *Steak*

| 22 | 14 | 18 | $40 |

Rumson | 21 W. River Rd. (Lafayette St.) | 732-842-6205 | www.whatsyourbeefrumsonnj.com

You "pick your own cut" then decide "how you want it cooked" at this longtime steakhouse "standard" in Rumson where "high-quality" chops and a "marvelous" salad bar keep regulars regular; "tired", "Elks Lodge"-esque decor, "long" weekend waits and a no-rezzie policy are the main beefs here.

	FOOD	DECOR	SERVICE	COST

☑ Whispers *American* — 27 | 24 | 26 | $58

Spring Lake | Hewitt Wellington Hotel | 200 Monmouth Ave. (2nd Ave.) | 732-974-9755 | www.whispersrestaurant.com

A bit of "heaven" in Spring Lake's Hewitt Wellington Hotel, this "romantic" BYO is "outstanding in every respect", starting with its "stellar" New American cooking and extending to its "spot-on" service and "elegant" Victorian inn setting; fans murmur it's "as good as it gets" for an "intimate candlelit dinner" with that special someone.

☑ White House *Sandwiches* — 26 | 8 | 16 | $14

Atlantic City | 2301 Arctic Ave. (Mississippi Ave.) | 609-345-1564 ⊞
Atlantic City | Trump Taj Mahal | 1000 Boardwalk (Virginia Ave.) | 609-345-7827 | www.trumptaj.com

"Ridiculously large" submarine sandwiches arrive on "paper plates" at this cash-only AC "institution" that's "always crowded" but certainly "worth the wait in line", despite "tacky" decor and "major attitude" from the staff; P.S. the spin-off in the Taj Mahal opened post-Survey.

Windansea *Seafood* — 17 | 19 | 19 | $38

Highlands | 56 Shrewsbury Ave. (Bay Ave.) | 732-872-2266 | www.windanseanj.com

"Great" views of the Shrewsbury River and Sandy Hook Bay trump the "solid if unspectacular" seafood slung at this "laid-back" Highlands "summer hangout"; "friendly" staffers, "surfer-chic" decor and a "popular bar scene" ratchet up the "cheery" vibe.

WindMill, The *Hot Dogs* — 19 | 8 | 14 | $12

Belmar | 1201 River Rd. (Rte. 71) | 732-681-9628 ◐
Long Branch | 200 Ocean Blvd. (Morris Ave.) | 732-870-6098
Long Branch | 586 Ocean Blvd. (Brighton Ave.) | 732-229-9863 ◐
Ocean Grove | 18 S. Main St. (Lake Ave.) | 732-988-5277
Red Bank | 22 N. Bridge Ave. (Front St.) | 732-747-5958
Brick | 856 Rte. 70 (Rte. 88) | 732-458-7774
www.windmillhotdogs.com

Nothing less than "Jersey Shore icons", these "decent" hot dog stands are known for their "crispy-skinned" red hots, not their "unattractive" looks and "counter-style service"; still, dog people say these "guilty pleasures" are just right when in the mood for cheap "seaside sustenance."

Wine Bar 🗷 Ⓜ *Eclectic/Mediterranean*

▽ 22 | 25 | 23 | $46

Atlantic Highlands | 40 First Ave. (Ocean Blvd.) | 732-291-1377 | www.ahwinebar.com

Oenophiles tout this "classy" second-story loft in Atlantic Highlands for its "wonderful" vino selection that makes the "delicious" Mediterranean-Eclectic food taste even better; the "romantic", "beautifully decorated" space includes French doors, "soft" chairs and a baby grand for cabaret shows.

Wolfgang Puck
American Grille *American*

23 | 23 | 23 | $56

Atlantic City | Borgata Hotel, Casino & Spa | 1 Borgata Way (Huron Ave.) | 609-317-1000 | www.theborgata.com

Marquee chef Puck lands in AC's Borgata Hotel with this "pleasurable dining experience" that "never disappoints" thanks to "creative" New Americana served by a "highly professional" crew in a room that's "relaxing" even though open to the casino; frugal folks who find the prices "way out of line" opt for the "tavern menu."

🗷 Yellow Fin *American*

27 | 18 | 21 | $59

Surf City | 104 24th St. (Long Beach Blvd.) | 609-494-7001

The tuna's "perfect" and all else is "consistently great" at this "artful" Surf City New American BYO that offers some of the "best dining" – for a "big-city" price – on LBI; despite "small" dimensions, "cramped" seating and "noisy" sound levels, it books up fast in season and is "worth it" for the "pulsing" vibe alone.

🗷 Yumi *Asian*

26 | 19 | 22 | $43

Sea Bright | 1120 Ocean Ave. (bet. Church & New Sts.) | 732-212-0881 | www.yumirestaurant.com

Downtown Sea Bright is home to this "delightful" Asian BYO known for its "amazing", "artistic" sushi and "large" menu of "beautifully prepared" cooked dishes; "courteous" staffers and a "well-appointed" setting help make it a "summer hot spot."

INDEXES

Cuisines

Includes names, locations and Food ratings.

AMERICAN

🆕 Aqua Blu | **Toms River**	‾
Atlantic B&G | **S Seaside Pk**	26
Avon Pavilion | **Avon-by-Sea**	19
Barnacle Bill's | **Rumson**	22
Basil T's | **Red Bank**	20
Bay Ave. | **Highlands**	28
🇿 Belford Bistro | **Belford**	26
Black-Eyed Susans | **Harvey Cedars**	‾
Black Trumpet | **Spring Lake**	24
Blue Pig | **Cape May**	21
Bonefish Grill | **multi.**	21
Brandl | **Belmar**	24
🆕 Breakfast Room | **A.C.**	‾
Brickwall Tavern | **Asbury Pk**	18
Cafe Loren | **Avalon**	25
Charley's | **Long Branch**	18
Chickie's/Pete's | **Egg Harbor Twp**	17
Copper Fish | **W Cape May**	20
Daddy O | **Long Beach**	19
Dauphin | **Asbury Pk**	22
David Burke | **Rumson**	25
Dish | **Red Bank**	25
🇿 Drew's Bayshore | **Keyport**	27
🇿 Ebbitt Room | **Cape May**	26
Inn/Sugar Hill | **Mays Landing**	18
🆕 JBJ Soul Kitchen | **Red Bank**	‾
L'assiette | **Surf City**	20
Lazy Dog Saloon | **Asbury Pk**	23
LoBianco | **Margate**	‾
Lucky Bones | **Cape May**	20
Mad Batter | **Cape May**	23
Matisse | **Belmar**	22
McLoone's | **multi.**	17
Merion Inn | **Cape May**	24
Mill/Spring Lake Hts. | **Spring Lake Hts**	21

Molly Pitcher Inn Restaurant | **Red Bank**	22
Moonstruck | **Asbury Pk**	25
Nauvoo Grill | **Fair Haven**	18
🇿 Nicholas | **Red Bank**	29
🆕 O Bistro | **A.C.**	‾
Old Man Rafferty's | **Asbury Pk**	18
🆕 Pacific Grill | **Wildwood**	‾
Peter Shields | **Cape May**	26
Plan B | **Asbury Pk**	24
Plantation | **Harvey Cedars**	18
Ram's Head Inn | **Galloway**	24
Raven/Peach | **Fair Haven**	24
Red | **Red Bank**	21
Remington's | **Manasquan**	21
Renault Winery | **Egg Harbor**	21
Rod's Olde Irish | **Sea Girt**	18
Sallee Tee's | **Monmouth Bch**	18
Salt Creek | **Rumson**	19
Scarborough Fair | **Sea Girt**	23
Shipwreck Grill | **Brielle**	24
Smithville Inn | **Smithville**	20
Spargo's | **Manalapan**	23
Steve/Cookie's | **Margate**	25
Grenville | **Bay Hd.**	17
Tim McLoone's | **Asbury Pk**	20
Tisha's | **Cape May**	25
Toast | **Asbury Pk**	22
Trinity | **Keyport**	25
Tun Tavern | **A.C.**	18
Ugly Mug | **Cape May**	15
Union Park | **Cape May**	25
🇿 Washington Inn | **Cape May**	28
🇿 Whispers | **Spring Lake**	27
Wolfgang Puck | **A.C.**	23
🇿 Yellow Fin | **Surf City**	27

ASIAN

Buddakan	**A.C.**	26
Teak	**Red Bank**	21

BARBECUE

Big Ed's BBQ	**Matawan**	18
D&L BBQ	**Bradley Bch**	24
Memphis Pig Out	**Atlantic Highlands**	19

BELGIAN

NEW Mussel Bar	**A.C.**	-

BURGERS

Barnacle Bill's	**Rumson**	22
Bobby's	**Eatontown**	21
Five Guys	**multi.**	21
WindMill	**multi.**	19

CAJUN

Trinity/Pope	**Asbury Pk**	21

CALIFORNIAN

Surf Taco	**multi.**	21
Tomatoes	**Margate**	25

CARIBBEAN

☑ 410 Bank St.	**Cape May**	26
Laila's	**Asbury Pk**	22

CHEESESTEAKS

Tony Luke's	**multi.**	20

CHINESE

(* dim sum specialist)

Crown Palace*	**Middletown**	20
Far East Taste	**Eatontown**	23
P.F. Chang's	**A.C.**	20
West Lake Seafood	**Matawan**	25

COFFEE SHOPS/ DINERS

Mustache Bill's	**Barnegat Light**	24
Teplitzky's	**A.C.**	18

COLOMBIAN

El Familiar	**Toms River**	-

CONTINENTAL

Daniel's Bistro	**Pt. Pleas. Bch**	-

CREOLE

Clementine's	**Avon-by-Sea**	23
☑ 410 Bank St.	**Cape May**	26
Trinity/Pope	**Asbury Pk**	21

CUBAN

NEW Cubacan	**Asbury Pk**	-
Cuba Libre	**A.C.**	21

DELIS

Richard's	**Long Branch**	20

DESSERT

Old Man Rafferty's	**Asbury Pk**	18

ECLECTIC

NEW Aqua Blu	**Toms River**	-
NEW Baia	**Somers Point**	-
Bistro/Red Bank	**Red Bank**	21
☑ Black Duck	**W Cape May**	26
Continental	**A.C.**	23
Eurasian	**Red Bank**	23
Gables	**Beach Haven**	24
Labrador	**Normandy Bch**	25
Langosta	**Asbury Pk**	22
Red Square	**A.C.**	21
Sallee Tee's	**Monmouth Bch**	18
Tomatoes	**Margate**	25
Wine Bar	**Atlantic Highlands**	22

FONDUE

Melting Pot	**multi.**	19

FRENCH

Claude's	**N Wildwood**	27

CUISINES

FRENCH (BISTRO)

Bienvenue | **Red Bank**	22
Le Fandy | **Fair Haven**	25

FRENCH (BRASSERIE)

Avenue | **Long Branch**	22

GERMAN

Alps Bistro | **Allentown**	-

GREEK

Athenian Gdn. | **Galloway Twp**	23
It's Greek To Me | **multi.**	18

HAWAIIAN

NEW Ohana Grill | **Lavallette**	-

HOT DOGS

WindMill | **multi.**	19

INDIAN

Aamantran | **Toms River**	21
Neelam | **Middletown**	20

IRISH

Irish Pub | **A.C.**	18

ITALIAN

(N=Northern; S=Southern)

Angelo's | **A.C.**	21
Anjelica's | S | **Sea Bright**	24
Anna's Kitchen | **Middletown**	23
NEW Baia | **Somers Point**	-
Barrels | **multi.**	21
Basil T's | **Red Bank**	20
Bay Ave. | **Highlands**	28
Bella Sogno | **Bradley Bch**	21
Capriccio | **A.C.**	25
Carmine's | **A.C.**	21
Z Chef Vola's | **A.C.**	26
Cucina Rosa | **Cape May**	21
Fornelletto | **A.C.**	24
Frescos | **Cape May**	22

Gaetano's | **Red Bank**	20
Z Girasole | S | **A.C.**	26
Z Il Mulino | **A.C.**	27
Jimmy's | S | **Asbury Pk**	23
NEW La Fontana Coast | **Sea Isle City**	-
La Pastaria | **Red Bank**	19
La Spiaggia | **Ship Bottom**	24
Luke Palladino | **multi.**	26
Z Mia | **A.C.**	26
Pete/Elda's | **Neptune City**	22
Piccola | **Ocean Twp**	26
Piero's | **Union Beach**	22
Portofino | **Tinton Falls**	24
Raimondo's | **Ship Bottom**	24
Roberto's | N | **Beach Haven**	21
San Remo | **Shrewsbury**	22
Sirena | **Long Branch**	23
Squan Tavern | S | **Manasquan**	20
Stella Marina | **Asbury Pk**	23
Tuzzio's | **Long Branch**	20
Undici | **Rumson**	22
Ventura's | **Margate**	18
Vic's | **Bradley Bch**	21
Villa Vittoria | **Brick**	23

JAPANESE

(* sushi specialist)

Aligado* | **Hazlet**	24
Benihana | **Toms River**	18
Ikko* | **Brick**	25
Izakaya | **A.C.**	23
Kanji* | **Tinton Falls**	24
Konbu* | **Manalapan**	26
Mahzu* | **Aberdeen**	20
Nobi* | **Toms River**	26
Sawa* | **multi.**	23
NEW Scarduzio's* | **A.C.**	-
Shogun* | **Toms River**	21
Sono* | **Middletown**	25
Sumo* | **Wall**	25

Taka*	**Asbury Pk**	25
Takara	**Oakhurst**	20
Wasabi*	**Matawan**	24
🌀 Yumi*	**Sea Bright**	26

MEDITERRANEAN

Frescos	**Cape May**	22
Moonstruck	**Asbury Pk**	25
Sage	**Ventnor**	25
Sofia	**Margate**	23
Wine Bar	**Atlantic Highlands**	22

MEXICAN

Aby's	**Matawan**	20
Baja Fresh	**Union Twp**	17
Chilangos	**Highlands**	21
NEW Dos Caminos	**A.C.**	-
El Familiar	**Toms River**	-
Jose's	**Spring Lake Hts**	23
Juanito's	**Red Bank**	23
Los Amigos	**A.C.**	23
Pop's Garage	**multi.**	22
Surf Taco	**multi.**	21

NUEVO LATINO

NEW Cubacan	**Asbury Pk**	-

PAN-LATIN

Casa Solar	**Belmar**	23

PIZZA

Grimaldi's	**Highlands**	25
Pete's/Elda's	**Neptune City**	22
Tony's Baltimore Grill	**A.C.**	18
Vic's	**Bradley Bch**	21

PORTUGUESE

Bistro Olé	**Asbury Pk**	23
Europa South	**Pt. Pleas. Bch**	21

PUB FOOD

Barnacle Bill's	**Rumson**	22
Brickwall Tavern	**Asbury Pk**	18

Chickie's/Pete's	**multi.**	17
Irish Pub	**A.C.**	18
Rod's Olde Irish	**Sea Girt**	18
Ugly Mug	**Cape May**	15

SANDWICHES

(See also Delis)

Sallee Tee's	**Monmouth Bch**	18
🌀 White House	**A.C.**	26

SEAFOOD

Allen's	**New Gretna**	22
Atlantic B&G	**S Seaside Pk**	26
Axelsson's	**Cape May**	23
Bahrs Landing	**Highlands**	17
Berkeley	**S Seaside Pk**	20
Bobby Chez	**multi.**	24
Bonefish Grill	**multi.**	21
Capt'n Ed's	**Pt. Pleas.**	20
NEW Chart House	**A.C.**	21
Copper Fish	**W Cape May**	20
Crab's Claw Inn	**Lavallette**	18
Crab Trap	**Somers Point**	21
Diving Horse	**Avalon**	24
🌀 Dock's	**A.C.**	26
Fin	**A.C.**	25
Harvey Cedars	**multi.**	23
Inlet Café	**Highlands**	20
Klein's	**Belmar**	19
Lobster House	**Cape May**	20
McCormick/Schmick	**A.C.**	20
Mill/Spring Lake Hts.	**Spring Lake Hts**	21
Mister C's/Bistro	**Allenhurst**	18
Mud City	**Manahawkin**	24
Navesink Fishery	**Navesink**	25
NEW Ohana Grill	**Lavallette**	-
Phillips Seafood	**A.C.**	20
Ray's	**Little Silver**	21
Red's Lobster	**Pt. Pleas. Bch**	24
Rooney's	**Long Branch**	19
SeaBlue	**A.C.**	26

CUISINES

Shipwreck Grill | **Brielle** 24
Spike's | **Pt. Pleas. Bch** 22
West Lake Seafood | **Matawan** 25
Windansea | **Highlands** 17

SMALL PLATES

Trinity/Pope | Cajun/Creole | **Asbury Pk** 21
Wine Bar | Eclectic/Med. | **Atlantic Highlands** 22

SOUTHWESTERN

Copper Canyon | **Atlantic Highlands** 23
Los Amigos | **A.C.** 23

SPANISH

Bistro Olé | **Asbury Pk** 23
Europa South | **Pt. Pleas. Bch** 21

STEAKHOUSES

Bobby Flay | **A.C.** 25
Brennen's | **Neptune City** 23
Capt'n Ed's | **Pt. Pleas.** 20
Chelsea Prime | **A.C.** 24
Danny's | **Red Bank** 20

Gallagher's | **A.C.** 22
Mill/Spring Lake Hts. | **Spring Lake Hts** 21
Morton's | **A.C.** 25
🔟 Old Homestead | **A.C.** 27
Ruth's Chris | **A.C.** 25
NEW Scarduzio's | **A.C.** -
Shipwreck Point | **Pt. Pleas. Bch** -
Shogun | **Toms River** 21
Simon Prime | **A.C.** -
Palm | **A.C.** 25
What's Your Beef? | **Rumson** 22

THAI

Aligado | **Hazlet** 24
Bamboo Leaf | **Bradley Bch** 22
Far East Taste | **Eatontown** 23
Siam Gdn. | **Red Bank** 24

VEGETARIAN

(* vegan)
Kaya's* | **Belmar** 24

VIETNAMESE

Bamboo Leaf | **Bradley Bch** 22
Little Saigon | **A.C.** 25

Locations

Includes names, cuisines and Food ratings.

Atlantic County

ATLANTIC CITY

Angelo's	*Italian*	21
Bobby Flay	*Steak*	25
NEW Breakfast Room	*Amer.*	–
Buddakan	*Asian*	26
Capriccio	*Italian*	25
Carmine's	*Italian*	21
NEW Chart House	*Seafood*	21
Z Chef Vola's	*Italian*	26
Chelsea Prime	*Steak*	24
Continental	*Eclectic*	23
Cuba Libre	*Cuban*	21
Z Dock's	*Seafood*	26
NEW Dos Caminos	*Mex.*	–
Fin	*Seafood*	25
Fornelletto	*Italian*	24
Gallagher's	*Steak*	22
Z Girasole	*Italian*	26
Z Il Mulino	*Italian*	27
Irish Pub	*Pub*	18
Izakaya	*Japanese*	23
Little Saigon	*Viet.*	25
Los Amigos	*Mex./SW*	23
Luke Palladino	*Italian*	26
McCormick/Schmick	*Seafood*	20
Melting Pot	*Fondue*	19
Z Mia	*Italian*	26
Morton's	*Steak*	25
NEW Mussel Bar	*Belgian*	–
NEW O Bistro	*Amer.*	–
Z Old Homestead	*Steak*	27
P.F. Chang's	*Chinese*	20
Phillips Seafood	*Seafood*	20
Red Square	*Eclectic*	21

Ruth's Chris	*Steak*	25
NEW Scarduzio's	*Japanese/Steak*	–
SeaBlue	*Seafood*	26
Simon Prime	*Steak*	–
Teplitzky's	*Diner*	18
Palm	*Steak*	25
Tony Luke's	*Cheesestks.*	20
Tony's Baltimore Grill	*Pizza*	18
Tun Tavern	*Amer.*	18
Z White House	*Sandwiches*	26
Wolfgang Puck	*Amer.*	23

EGG HARBOR

Bonefish Grill	*Seafood*	21
Chickie's/Pete's	*Pub*	17
Renault Winery	*Amer.*	21

GALLOWAY

Ram's Head Inn	*Amer.*	24

GALLOWAY TOWNSHIP

Athenian Gdn.	*Greek*	23

LINWOOD

Barrels	*Italian*	21

MARGATE

Barrels	*Italian*	21
Bobby Chez	*Seafood*	24
LoBianco	*Amer.*	–
Sofia	*Med.*	23
Steve/Cookie's	*Amer.*	25
Tomatoes	*Cal./Eclectic*	25
Ventura's	*Italian*	18

MAYS LANDING

Bobby Chez	*Seafood*	24
Inn/Sugar Hill	*Amer.*	18

LOCATIONS

NORTHFIELD

Luke Palladino | Italian   26

SMITHVILLE

Smithville Inn | Amer.   20

SOMERS POINT

NEW Baia | Italian   -
Crab Trap | Seafood   21

VENTNOR

Sage | Med.   25

Burlington County

NEW GRETNA

Allen's | Seafood   22

Cape May County

AVALON

Cafe Loren | Amer.   25
Diving Horse | Seafood   24

CAPE MAY

Axelsson's | Seafood   23
Blue Pig | Amer.   21
Cucina Rosa | Italian   21
Z Ebbitt Room | Amer.   26
Z 410 Bank St. | 26
  Carib./Creole
Frescos | Italian/Med.   22
Lobster House | Seafood   20
Lucky Bones | Amer.   20
Mad Batter | Amer.   23
Merion Inn | Amer.   24
Peter Shields | Amer.   26
Tisha's | Amer.   25
Ugly Mug | Pub   15
Union Park | Amer.   25
Z Washington Inn | Amer.   28

NORTH WILDWOOD

Claude's | French   27

OCEAN CITY

Chickie's/Pete's | Pub   17

SEA ISLE CITY

NEW La Fontana Coast | Italian   -

WEST CAPE MAY

Z Black Duck | Eclectic   26
Copper Fish | Amer./Seafood   20

WILDWOOD

Chickie's/Pete's | Pub   17
NEW Pacific Grill | Amer.   -
Tony Luke's | Cheesestks.   20

Monmouth County

ABERDEEN

Mahzu | Japanese   20

ALLENHURST

Mister C's/Bistro | Seafood   18

ALLENTOWN

Alps Bistro | German   -

ASBURY PARK

Bistro Olé | Portug./Spanish   23
Brickwall Tavern | Pub   18
NEW Cubacan | Cuban   -
Dauphin | Amer.   22
Jimmy's | Italian   23
Laila's | Carib.   22
Langosta | Eclectic   22
Lazy Dog Saloon | Amer.   23
McLoone's | Amer.   17
Moonstruck | Amer./Med.   25
Old Man Rafferty's | Amer.   18
Plan B | Amer.   24
Pop's Garage | Mex.   22
Stella Marina | Italian   23

Taka | *Japanese* 25
Tim McLoone's | *Amer.* 20
Toast | *Amer.* 22
Trinity/Pope | *Cajun/Creole* 21

ATLANTIC HIGHLANDS

Copper Canyon | *SW* 23
Memphis Pig Out | *BBQ* 19
Wine Bar | *Eclectic/Med.* 22

AVON-BY-THE-SEA

Avon Pavilion | *Amer.* 19
Clementine's | *Creole* 23

BELFORD

🅕 Belford Bistro | *Amer.* 26

BELMAR

Brandl | *Amer.* 24
Casa Solar | *Pan-Latin* 23
Kaya's | *Veg.* 24
Klein's | *Seafood* 19
Matisse | *Amer.* 22
Surf Taco | *Mex.* 21
WindMill | *Hot Dogs* 19

BRADLEY BEACH

Bamboo Leaf | *Thai/Viet.* 22
Bella Sogno | *Italian* 21
D&L BBQ | *BBQ* 24
Vic's | *Italian/Pizza* 21

BRIELLE

Shipwreck Grill | *Amer./Seafood* 24

EATONTOWN

Bobby's | *Burgers* 21
Far East Taste | *Chinese/Thai* 23
Sawa | *Japanese* 23

FAIR HAVEN

Le Fandy | *French* 25
Nauvoo Grill | *Amer.* 18
Raven/Peach | *Amer.* 24

HAZLET

Aligado | *Thai* 24

HIGHLANDS

Bahrs Landing | *Seafood* 17
Bay Ave. | *Amer./Italian* 28
Chilangos | *Mex.* 21
Grimaldi's | *Pizza* 25
Inlet Café | *Seafood* 20
Windansea | *Seafood* 17

HOLMDEL

It's Greek To Me | *Greek* 18

KEYPORT

🅕 Drew's Bayshore | *Amer.* 27
Trinity | *Amer.* 25

LITTLE SILVER

Ray's | *Seafood* 21

LONG BRANCH

Avenue | *French* 22
Charley's | *Amer.* 18
It's Greek To Me | *Greek* 18
McLoone's | *Amer.* 17
Richard's | *Deli* 20
Rooney's | *Seafood* 19
Sawa | *Japanese* 23
Sirena | *Italian* 23
Surf Taco | *Mex.* 21
WindMill | *Hot Dogs* 19
Tuzzio's | *Italian* 20

MANALAPAN

Konbu | *Japanese* 26
Spargo's | *Amer.* 23

MANASQUAN

Remington's | *Amer.* 21
Squan Tavern | *Italian* 20
Surf Taco | *Mex.* 21

MATAWAN

Aby's	*Mex.*	20
Big Ed's BBQ	*BBQ*	18
Wasabi	*Japanese*	24
West Lake Seafood	*Chinese*	25

MIDDLETOWN

Anna's Kitchen	*Italian*	23
Crown Palace	*Chinese*	20
Neelam	*Indian*	20
Sono	*Japanese*	25

MONMOUTH BEACH

Sallee Tee's	*Amer./Eclectic*	18

NAVESINK

Navesink Fishery	*Seafood*	25

NEPTUNE CITY

Brennen's	*Steak*	23
Pete/Elda's	*Pizza*	22

OAKHURST/ OCEAN TOWNSHIP

Piccola	*Italian*	26
Takara	*Japanese*	20

OCEAN GROVE

WindMill	*Hot Dogs*	19

RED BANK

Basil T's	*Amer./Italian*	20
Bienvenue	*French*	22
Bistro/Red Bank	*Eclectic*	21
Bonefish Grill	*Seafood*	21
Danny's	*Steak*	20
Dish	*Amer.*	25
Eurasian	*Eclectic*	23
Gaetano's	*Italian*	20
NEW JBJ Soul Kitchen	*Amer.*	-
Juanito's	*Mex.*	23
La Pastaria	*Italian*	19
Melting Pot	*Fondue*	19

Molly Pitcher Inn Restaurant	*Amer.*	22
🔁 Nicholas	*Amer.*	29
Red	*Amer.*	21
Siam Gdn.	*Thai*	24
Surf Taco	*Mex.*	21
Teak	*Asian*	21
WindMill	*Hot Dogs*	19

RUMSON

Barnacle Bill's	*Burgers*	22
David Burke	*Amer.*	25
Salt Creek	*Amer.*	19
Undici	*Italian*	22
What's Your Beef?	*Steak*	22

SEA BRIGHT

Anjelica's	*Italian*	24
McLoone's	*Amer.*	17
🔁 Yumi	*Asian*	26

SEA GIRT

Rod's Olde Irish	*Pub*	18
Scarborough Fair	*Amer.*	23

SHREWSBURY

Pop's Garage	*Mex.*	22
San Remo	*Italian*	22

SPRING LAKE

Black Trumpet	*Amer.*	24
🔁 Whispers	*Amer.*	27

SPRING LAKE HEIGHTS

Jose's	*Mex.*	23
Mill/Spring Lake Hts.	*Amer.*	21

TINTON FALLS

Kanji	*Japanese*	24
Portofino	*Italian*	24

UNION BEACH

Piero's	*Italian*	22

WALL

Sumo | *Japanese*   25

Delaware Valley

UNION TOWNSHIP

Baja Fresh | *Mex.*   17

Ocean County

BARNEGAT LIGHT

Mustache Bill's | *Diner*   24

BAY HEAD

Grenville | *Amer.*   17

BEACH HAVEN

Gables | *Eclectic*   24
Harvey Cedars | *Seafood*   23
Roberto's | *Italian*   21

BRICK

Bonefish Grill | *Seafood*   21
Five Guys | *Burgers*   21
Ikko | *Japanese*   25
WindMill | *Hot Dogs*   19
Villa Vittoria | *Italian*   23

FORKED RIVER

Surf Taco | *Mex.*   21

HARVEY CEDARS

Black-Eyed Susans | *Amer.*   -
Harvey Cedars | *Seafood*   23
Plantation | *Amer.*   18

LAVALLETTE

Crab's Claw Inn | *Seafood*   18
NEW Ohana Grill | -
  Hawaiian/Seafood

LONG BEACH TOWNSHIP

Daddy O | *Amer.*   19

MANAHAWKIN

Mud City | *Seafood*   24

NORMANDY BEACH

Labrador | *Eclectic*   25
Pop's Garage | *Mex.*   22

POINT PLEASANT

Capt'n Ed's | *Seafood/Steak*   20

POINT PLEASANT BEACH

Daniel's Bistro | *Continental*   -
Europa South | *Portug./Spanish*   21
Red's Lobster | *Seafood*   24
Shipwreck Point | *Steak*   -
Spike's | *Seafood*   22
Surf Taco | *Mex.*   21

SHIP BOTTOM

La Spiaggia | *Italian*   24
Raimondo's | *Italian*   24

SOUTH SEASIDE PARK

Atlantic B&G | *Amer./Seafood*   26
Berkeley | *Seafood*   20

SURF CITY

L'assiette | *Amer.*   20
Z Yellow Fin | *Amer.*   27

TOMS RIVER

Aamantran | *Indian*   21
NEW Aqua Blu | *Amer.*   -
Benihana | *Japanese*   18
El Familiar | *Colombian/Mex.*   -
Five Guys | *Burgers*   21
Nobi | *Japanese*   26
Shogun | *Japanese/Steak*   21
Surf Taco | *Mex.*   21

Special Features

Listings cover the best in each category and include names, locations and Food ratings. Multi-location restaurants' features may vary by branch.

ADDITIONS

(Properties added since the last edition of the book)

Alps Bistro | **Allentown**	⌐
Aqua Blu | **Toms River**	⌐
Baia | **Somers Point**	⌐
Black-Eyed Susans | **Harvey Cedars**	⌐
Breakfast Room | **A.C.**	⌐
Cubacan | **Asbury Pk**	⌐
Dos Caminos | **A.C.**	⌐
JBJ Soul Kitchen | **Red Bank**	⌐
La Fontana Coast | **Sea Isle City**	⌐
LoBianco | **Margate**	⌐
Mussel Bar | **A.C.**	⌐
O Bistro | **A.C.**	⌐
Ohana Grill | **Lavallette**	⌐
Pacific Grill | **Wildwood**	⌐
Scarduzio's | **A.C.**	⌐

BREAKFAST

(See also Hotel Dining)

Avon Pavilion | **Avon-by-Sea**	19
Mustache Bill's | **Barnegat Light**	24
Tisha's | **Cape May**	25

BRUNCH

Crown Palace | **Middletown**	20
David Burke | **Rumson**	25
Gables | **Beach Haven**	24
Matisse | **Belmar**	22
Molly Pitcher Inn Restaurant | **Red Bank**	22
West Lake Seafood | **Matawan**	25

HOTEL DINING

Atlantic City Hilton
Simon Prime | **A.C.**	⌐

Berkeley Hotel
Dauphin | **Asbury Pk**	22

Blue Bay Inn
Copper Canyon | **Atlantic Highlands**	23

Borgata Hotel, Casino & Spa
Bobby Flay | **A.C.**	25
Fornelletto | **A.C.**	24
Izakaya | **A.C.**	23
⊠ Old Homestead | **A.C.**	27
SeaBlue | **A.C.**	26
Tony Luke's | **A.C.**	20
Wolfgang Puck | **A.C.**	23

Caesars on the Boardwalk
⊠ Mia | **A.C.**	26

Carroll Villa Hotel
Mad Batter | **Cape May**	23

Chelsea Hotel
Chelsea Prime | **A.C.**	24
Teplitzky's | **A.C.**	18

Congress Hall Hotel
Blue Pig | **Cape May**	21

Daddy O Hotel
Daddy O | **Long Beach**	19

Gables Inn
Gables | **Beach Haven**	24

Golden Nugget Hotel & Casino
NEW Chart House | **A.C.**	21

Grand Victorian Hotel
Black Trumpet | **Spring Lake**	24

Grenville Hotel
Grenville | **Bay Hd.**	17

Harrah's
NEW Dos Caminos | **A.C.**	⌐
Luke Palladino | **A.C.**	26
McCormick/Schmick | **A.C.**	20

Hewitt Wellington Hotel
  Ⓩ Whispers | **Spring Lake**   27

Macomber, Hotel
  Union Park | **Cape May**   25

Molly Pitcher Inn
  Molly Pitcher Inn Restaurant | 22
  Red Bank

Ocean Club Condos
  Ⓩ Girasole | **A.C.**   26

Quarter at the Tropicana
  Carmine's | **A.C.**   21
  Cuba Libre | **A.C.**   21
  P.F. Chang's | **A.C.**   20
  Red Square | **A.C.**   21
  Palm | **A.C.**   25

Resorts Casino & Hotel
  Capriccio | **A.C.**   25
  Gallagher's | **A.C.**   22

Revel
  NEW Breakfast Room | **A.C.**   –
  NEW Mussel Bar | **A.C.**   –
  NEW O Bistro | **A.C.**   –

Sheraton Atlantic City
  Tun Tavern | **A.C.**   18

Showboat Casino
  NEW Scarduzio's | **A.C.**   –

Tropicana Casino & Resort
  Fin | **A.C.**   25

Trump Taj Mahal
  Ⓩ Il Mulino | **A.C.**   27

Virginia Hotel
  Ⓩ Ebbitt Room | **Cape May**   26

OUTDOOR DINING

(G=garden; P=patio; S=sidewalk;
T=Terrace)

NEW Aqua Blu | P | **Toms River**   –
Atlantic B&G | P | **S Seaside Pk**   26
Avenue | T | **Long Branch**   22
Avon Pavilion | T | **Avon-by-Sea**   19
Axelsson's | G | **Cape May**   23
NEW Baia | T | **Somers Point**   –

Bamboo Leaf | S | **Bradley Bch**   22
Bobby Chez | P | **Margate**   24
Danny's | S | **Red Bank**   20
Diving Horse | P | **Avalon**   24
Gables | P | **Beach Haven**   24
Ⓩ Girasole | P | **A.C.**   26
Klein's | P, T | **Belmar**   19
NEW La Fontana Coast | P | –
  Sea Isle City
Matisse | T | **Belmar**   22
Mill/Spring Lake Hts. | T | 21
  Spring Lake Hts
Moonstruck | T | **Asbury Pk**   25
Peter Shields | T | **Cape May**   26
Raven/Peach | P | **Fair Haven**   24
Shipwreck Grill | T | **Brielle**   24
Sirena | T | **Long Branch**   23
Sofia | G, P, T | **Margate**   23
Stella Marina | P | **Asbury Pk**   23
Tisha's | P | **Cape May**   25
Windansea | T | **Highlands**   17

VIEWS

NEW Aqua Blu | **Toms River**   –
Atlantic B&G | **S Seaside Pk**   26
Avenue | **Long Branch**   22
Avon Pavilion | **Avon-by-Sea**   19
Bahrs Landing | **Highlands**   17
NEW Baia | **Somers Point**   –
Barnacle Bill's | **Rumson**   22
Berkeley | **S Seaside Pk**   20
Buddakan | **A.C.**   26
Capriccio | **A.C.**   25
Charley's | **Long Branch**   18
Chelsea Prime | **A.C.**   24
Chickie's/Pete's | **Wildwood**   17
Continental | **A.C.**   23
Crab Trap | **Somers Point**   21
NEW Cubacan | **Asbury Pk**   –
NEW Dos Caminos | **A.C.**   –
Inlet Café | **Highlands**   20

🆕 La Fontana Coast | **Sea Isle City**	–
Langosta | **Asbury Pk**	22
Matisse | **Belmar**	22
McLoone's | **multi.**	17
Mill/Spring Lake Hts. | **Spring Lake Hts**	21
Mister C's/Bistro | **Allenhurst**	18
Molly Pitcher Inn Restaurant | **Red Bank**	22
Moonstruck | **Asbury Pk**	25
🆕 O Bistro | **A.C.**	–
Phillips Seafood | **A.C.**	20
Plantation | **Harvey Cedars**	18
Rooney's | **Long Branch**	19
Sallee Tee's | **Monmouth Bch**	18
Salt Creek | **Rumson**	19
Sawa | **Long Branch**	23
Shipwreck Point | **Pt. Pleas. Bch**	–
Sirena | **Long Branch**	23
Smithville Inn | **Smithville**	20
Sofia | **Margate**	23
Stella Marina | **Asbury Pk**	23
Tim McLoone's | **Asbury Pk**	20
Union Park | **Cape May**	25
Ventura's | **Margate**	18
Windansea | **Highlands**	17

WATERSIDE

🆕 Aqua Blu | **Toms River**	–
Atlantic B&G | **S Seaside Pk**	26
Avenue | **Long Branch**	22
Avon Pavilion | **Avon-by-Sea**	19

Axelsson's | **Cape May**	23
Bahrs Landing | **Highlands**	17
🆕 Baia | **Somers Point**	–
Barnacle Bill's | **Rumson**	22
Capriccio | **A.C.**	25
Chickie's/Pete's | **Wildwood**	17
Crab Trap | **Somers Point**	21
Fin | **A.C.**	25
Inlet Café | **Highlands**	20
Inn/Sugar Hill | **Mays Landing**	18
It's Greek To Me | **Long Branch**	18
Klein's | **Belmar**	19
Langosta | **Asbury Pk**	22
Matisse | **Belmar**	22
McLoone's | **multi.**	17
Mill/Spring Lake Hts. | **Spring Lake Hts**	21
Mister C's/Bistro | **Allenhurst**	18
Molly Pitcher Inn Restaurant | **Red Bank**	22
Peter Shields | **Cape May**	26
Pop's Garage | **Asbury Pk**	22
Red's Lobster | **Pt. Pleas. Bch**	24
Rooney's | **Long Branch**	19
Sallee Tee's | **Monmouth Bch**	18
Sirena | **Long Branch**	23
Stella Marina | **Asbury Pk**	23
Teplitzky's | **A.C.**	18
Tim McLoone's | **Asbury Pk**	20
Union Park | **Cape May**	25
Ventura's | **Margate**	18
Windansea | **Highlands**	17